TOPICS TODAY

T0003703

Racism and Racial Justice

By Sophie Washburne

Cavendish Square

New York

Published in 2021 by Cavendish Square Publishing, LLC
243 5th Avenue, Suite 136, New York, NY 10016

Copyright © 2021 by Cavendish Square Publishing, LLC

First Edition

Website: cavendishsq.com

This publication represents the opinions and views of the author based on his or her personal experience, knowledge, and research. The information in this book serves as a general guide only. The author and publisher have used their best efforts in preparing this book and disclaim liability rising directly or indirectly from the use and application of this book.

Portions of this work were originally authored by David Robson and published as *Racism* (*Hot Topics*). All new material this edition authored by Sophie Washburne.

All websites were available and accurate when this book was sent to press.

Library of Congress Cataloging-in-Publication Data

Names: Washburne, Sophie, author.
Title: Racism and Racial Justice / Sophie Washburne.
Description: New York : Cavendish Square Publishing, [2021] | Series: Topics today | Includes bibliographical references and index.
Identifiers: LCCN 2020007267 (print) | LCCN 2020007268 (ebook) | ISBN 9781502657510 (library binding) | ISBN 9781502657503 (paperback) | ISBN 9781502657527 (ebook)
Subjects: LCSH: Racism–United States–History–Juvenile literature. | United States–Race relations–History–Juvenile literature.
Classification: LCC E184.A1 W263 2021 (print) | LCC E184.A1 (ebook) | DDC 305.800973–dc23
LC record available at https://lccn.loc.gov/2020007267
LC ebook record available at https://lccn.loc.gov/2020007268

Editor: Jennifer Lombardo
Copy Editor: Michelle Denton
Designer: Deanna Paternostro

Some of the images in this book illustrate individuals who are models. The depictions do not imply actual situations or events.

CPSIA compliance information: Batch #CS20CSQ: For further information contact Cavendish Square Publishing LLC, New York, New York, at 1-877-980-4450.

Printed in China

Find us on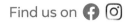

A LONG HISTORY OF HATE

Racism, or the belief that some races are better than others, has been around for centuries, but it's still a relatively modern concept. Race is a social construct, which means humans made it up. Genetically, there's very little difference between humans, and skin color doesn't determine someone's personality or talents. In ancient societies, people were more likely to be discriminated against based on things such as their religion or language. For instance, in ancient Rome and Greece, people of any race could be sold into slavery. Although race is a social construct, discrimination based on perceived race is very real. In many cases, people with lighter skin are the ones who benefit most from this system, even if the individuals aren't actively trying to oppress people with darker skin. In the United States, white people are the group with the most power and privilege.

However, "lighter" doesn't just mean "white." Also, racism is not a problem that is unqiue to the United States. For example, in Singapore, Chinese are the majority race, and they have displayed racism toward Singaporeans of ethnicities with darker skin tones. In 2019, *Business Insider* published a report stating that half of all Malays—an ethnic group from Malaysia—and Indians say they feel discriminated against when they apply for jobs in Singapore. Some housing ads state that certain races, including Indian and Malay, aren't welcome; even when this isn't explicitly stated, people of these ethnicities report being told

◀ Racism is a global issue. As a minority ethnic group, Malays have often experienced racism and discrimination in Singapore.

that a landlord won't rent to them. Other studies have found that Malays, in particular, are excluded from holding certain military positions. They have repeatedly requested more equal treatment in this area and have been denied by the Singaporean government.

Malays have also been subject to some of the same damaging stereotypes people have used to label and oppress certain groups throughout history. For instance, people—especially white people—have often applied the label of "lazy" to Malays, African Americans, Native Americans, Aboriginal Australians, the Maori people of New Zealand, and more. Implying that people who belong to these groups don't want to work hard gives the group in power an excuse not to give them jobs, equal pay, financial support from the government, and other rights and opportunities that would put these disadvantaged groups on an equal footing with the group in power.

Racism in America

The history of racism in the United States is long and painful. The first British settlement in what would later become the United States was founded in Jamestown, Virginia, in 1607, but the British were far from alone. By the early 1600s, the Spanish, French, and Dutch had all claimed portions of North America. However, each of these groups of white Europeans could only maintain their colonies by persecuting the Native Americans who were already living there when the settlers arrived. They took Native American lands, broke treaties, and actively attempted to exterminate the various native groups, all in the name of expanding their empires.

After the United States became an independent country, this persecution became national policy. Most notably, in the 1830s, the US government forced the Cherokee people to move from present-day Georgia, Tennessee, Alabama, North Carolina, and Florida to present-day Oklahoma so Southerners could settle and plant crops where the Cherokee had once lived. This journey was often difficult and dangerous, and many people died on the way, which led to this event being called the Trail of Tears. Today, negative, racist attitudes regarding Native Americans and their lands still exist.

Black people have also had an especially difficult time in the United States from the beginning. In 1619, the first slaves were brought from Africa to the colony of Virginia. Slavery became a national institution and, although it was eventually abolished, racist attitudes against black people persist throughout the country.

As time went on and people from other countries began immigrating to the United States, they, too, often faced racism or prejudice when they arrived. Although people of typically white nationalities, such as the Irish and Italians, were discriminated against, this was not due to the color of their skin, and they were eventually able to assimilate into, or become part of, the mainstream culture in the United States. However, for Africans, Arabs, Middle Easterners, Latin Americans, East Asians, and Southeast Asians, their skin color has made them easy targets for discrimination and sometimes violence.

A Lasting Problem

When Barack Obama was elected president of the United States in 2008, many people took this as proof that racism no longer existed in the United States. However, despite the feelings of hope surrounding Obama's historic election, racism still existed in the United States and around the world. For example, in the early days of Obama's campaign, Secret Service agents, charged with guarding the president and presidential candidates, investigated death threats, many of which mentioned his race, on an almost daily basis. After Obama's inauguration in January 2009, death threats against him soared, with the Secret Service fielding at least 30 each day—much higher than those against any other president.

The emergence of the Black Lives Matter (BLM) movement in 2013 was one response to the racism that black people still experience in America today. However, even after seeing multiple news stories and videos in which unarmed black people were the victims of police brutality, some people still denied that racism was real. Some people have difficulty recognizing systemic, or institutional, racism, which is racism that is "structured into political and social institutions. It occurs when [organizations], institutions or governments discriminate, either deliberately or indirectly, against

People of color are disproportionately likely to be arrested or put in prison.

certain groups of people to limit their rights."[1]

Racism most frequently refers to discrimination based on skin color, but other traits can cause people to experience a similar type of discrimination. For example, Jewish and Latinx people don't belong to any one race, but these groups have effectively been racialized, especially in the United States. Members of these groups often feel a common bond with each other, and Latinx people in particular often consider their ethnicity to be part of their racial identity. Andrea Alvarez, curatorial assistant at the Albright-Knox Art Gallery in Buffalo, New York, explained, "I think the prejudice that people experience in the Latinx and Hispanic communities is sometimes based on race, but it's more often about the place of origin rather than the color of their skin specifically. What seems to be the main fear isn't the racial difference but the nature of the movement of people, the social structures, the threat to national language, etc., which people don't associate with any one 'race' from Latin America but instead associate with the migration pattern."[2]

One of the most glaring examples of systemic racism in America today is the number of young black and Latino men in prison compared to the number of white men. For example, although only about 12 percent of drug users are black, almost 30 percent of people arrested for drug charges are black. This statistic points out a vast difference in the way black and white people are treated by the judicial system, as two scholars explained:

> *Although no longer inscribed in law, [racism] is implicit to processes of law enforcement, prosecution, and incarceration, guiding the behavior of police, prosecutors, judges, juries, wardens, and parole boards. Hence, African Americans continue to experience higher rates of incarceration than do whites charged with similar crimes, endure longer sentences for the same classes of crimes perpetrated by whites, and, compared to white inmates, receive far less consideration by parole boards when being considered for release.*[3]

Although racism against black people in particular is often in the news, this is not the only group that is discriminated against. During Donald Trump's 2016 presidential campaign, he verbally attacked undocumented Mexican immigrants, claiming that many who came to the United States were criminals. After Trump was elected, the number of hate crimes against people who didn't appear to be white rose dramatically.

Some groups, such as Native American and Asian American people, are often ignored by the media, but this doesn't mean they don't experience racism. It simply means the racism is hidden, which makes it harder to fight. Learning about racism and the distressing effects it has on its victims is the first step toward ending it and creating a new system of racial justice—one that gives all people, regardless of race, equal rights, power, and opportunities.

CHAPTER ONE

WHAT DOES RACISM LOOK LIKE?

Racism seems straightforward, but it can be surprisingly complex. Some people deny that it exists or falsely claim that the group in power is actually the one oppressed by minority groups. Others will acknowledge that an action is racist only if it's very obvious, but deny that anything subtle is racism. For instance, few people will defend a white person who openly states that they won't hire black people, but if a black person says they feel discriminated against in the hiring process, some people will say they're imagining things.

Racism involves prejudice, or negative opinions, judgments, and attitudes about people based on their race. David T. Wellman, author of *Portraits of White Racism*, explained that racism is more than just bias against a group of people based on skin color. Rather, Wellman defined racism as a "system of advantage based on race."[1] In other words, racism involves not only discriminating against one race but also upholding the advantages another race enjoys, including better opportunities for education, housing, and employment.

In the past, people were often more openly racist. Advertisements that used racial stereotypes to sell products were common, as were racial slurs, which are insulting nicknames for people of a certain race. After the civil rights movement of

The Ku Klux Klan (KKK) is one of the oldest hate groups in the United States. It was founded after the American Civil War to stop black people from exercising their rights, and it's still active today. Members often wear white robes and hoods.

the 1950s and 1960s, attitudes regarding racism slowly began to change. Unfortunately, racism did not disappear; it simply became less acceptable to speak about openly. In modern society, the general population often views openly racist acts as shocking, while subtly racist acts often go unnoticed or even defended by those who aren't victims themselves.

Hate Crimes and Hate Groups

Racism is often violent. Acts of violence or vandalism against a person because of their race, ethnicity, religion, or sexual orientation are called hate crimes, and thousands of people are victims each year. In the United States, 5,818 single-bias hate crimes were reported in 2015. This was a small increase from 2014, when 5,462 single-bias hate crimes were reported. Single-bias means there was only one motivating factor for the crime. Some hate crimes involve multiple prejudices; for example, someone might be attacked because they are both black and disabled. Police determined that about 57 percent of the reported single-bias hate crimes in 2015 were racially motivated. The day after the 2016 presidential election, the number of reported hate crimes rose dramatically, with 202 incidents reported on November 9 alone. According to *Forbes* magazine, "Many of those incidents involved harassers invoking Trump's name, making it clear that the outbreak of hate was primarily due to his success in the election."[2] By the end of 2016, the total number of single-bias hate crimes was at 6,063, with 57.5 percent motivated by race. This number has kept climbing throughout Trump's presidency. In 2017, 7,106 single-bias crimes were reported, and in 2018, the total was 8,327.

Nonwhite immigrants, black people, and Jewish people are primary targets for hate crimes. Anti-immigrant sentiments increased during Trump's campaign as he blamed Mexican and Muslim people for many of America's safety concerns. When people speak negatively about immigrants, they generally mean people who aren't white. Although white people who come from Europe to live in the United States are also immigrants, there's little, if any, negative feeling toward them from the general population.

Judaism is a religion, not a race. However, anti-Semitism—hostility toward Jewish people—often appears the same as racism.

According to a poll by Morning Consult, a neutral media and technology company, many Americans favor immigrants from Europe and Asia over those from other countries.

Hate crimes are not generally crimes committed by one person acting alone. Some perpetrators identify themselves as members of an organized group. The Southern Poverty Law Center (SPLC), a nonprofit social justice group, identified 892 active hate groups in the United States in 2015, up from 784 the previous year. In this area, too, the upward trend has continued: By 2018, the SPLC was tracking 1,020 hate groups across the country. According to the organization, this is a record number that represents an increase of

30 percent since 2014. Although not all of these groups are known to be violent, sociologists argue that their very presence can spark violent acts of racism.

An International Problem

While thousands of racially motivated crimes are committed in the United States each year, other countries are not immune to the phenomenon. Finland, England, Ireland, China, Greece, Sweden, Denmark, Germany, Spain, and France are but a few of the countries where this kind of violence has risen. In June 2016, the United Kingdom (UK)—England, Northern Ireland, Wales, and Scotland—voted to leave the European Union (EU). This became known as Brexit, a combination of the words "Britain" and "exit." One major motivation for those who voted to leave was to make it harder for immigrants to enter the country. As with Trump's election, after Brexit, the number of hate crimes rose dramatically. British police reported a 57 percent increase in hate crimes in the four days after the first Brexit vote. However, unlike in the United States, even white immigrants are being targeted in the UK.

In Europe and South America particularly, soccer fans regularly show their racist tendencies. Amid the cheers and boos typical of any sporting event, extreme fans known as hooligans frequently shout racial insults, throw garbage, and make monkey noises at black players—implying that people of color resemble monkeys. Many of the fans consider the behavior little more than a show of enthusiasm for their own team. "The kids' chanting last night was stupid but harmless," said Alejandro, a Spanish soccer (also known as football) fan, after one such event. "Football is always about insulting the other team. The racism wasn't meant seriously."[3]

Italy has a population of more than 60 million people. However, millions of immigrants reside there illegally. Italy depends on undocumented immigrants, who are mostly from West Africa, to work long hours for very little pay picking fruit, a job many Italians consider beneath them. In January 2010, some of the country's worst race riots in years erupted after two African immigrants were shot and wounded with a pellet gun in the southern region of

Soccer matches in Europe frequently get out of hand. Sometimes violent incidents similar to this one are racially charged.

Calabria. Other African immigrants, who blamed racism for the attack, took to the streets in protest, throwing rocks, setting cars on fire, and clashing with local police. More than 50 immigrants and police officers were wounded in the two days of rioting that engulfed the entire city of Rosarno.

The incident revealed the ugly reality of Italy's dependence on cheap labor and the racism that's often involved. "This event pulled the lid off something that we who work in the sector know well but no one talks about: That many Italian economic realities are based on the exploitation of low-cost foreign labor, living in subhuman conditions, without human rights,"[4] said Flavio di Giacomo, spokesperson for the International Organization for Migration.

Racism in the Workplace

Racism isn't always expressed through violent actions. Racial discrimination, although typically illegal, remains common in many countries, and the United States is no exception. In 2010 alone, 35,890 cases of racial discrimination in the workplace were filed with the US Equal Employment Opportunity Commission (EEOC), which is responsible for enforcing federal laws against discrimination. That year represented the peak number of cases filed in the new millennium. Since then, the number has generally been decreasing, although there have been spikes in certain years. In 2019, 23,976 cases of racial discrimination were filed. Such cases are

Problems with Investigating Workplace Discrimination

In addition to the difficulty of proving discrimination, people trying to file claims with the EEOC face the issue of the department's understaffing and underfunding. Vox explained:

Since 2008, the EEOC has doubled the share of complaints involving companies or local government agencies that it places on its lowest-priority track, effectively guaranteeing no probes, mediation, or other substantive efforts on behalf of those workers ... The EEOC said it has focused its limited resources "on charges where the government can have the greatest impact on workplace discrimination." But as it cuts its backlog [cases waiting for resolution] by 30 percent in the last decade ... the already-low share of workers getting help has dropped. Only 13 percent of all complaints the EEOC closed [in 2018] ended with a settlement or other relief for the workers who filed them, down from 18 percent in 2008 ...

Gabrielle Martin, a 30-year EEOC attorney and president of the National Council of EEOC Locals No. 216, said the agency's decision to send more cases to the "killing fields"—

frequently difficult to prove, but some have gone to court. For example, in 2019, the EEOC sued an Indiana company called Coffel Vending after a black job applicant with many years of experience proved that he had been denied a job due to his race.

Racial discrimination occurs in the workplace when a person is prevented from holding a certain job or from advancing in their career because of their race. Discriminatory practices in the workplace are reflected in the income disparity, or difference, between people of color and white people in the United States. According to data from the US Census Bureau, black families earn on average only about $104,000 per year and Latinx families earn about $103,000,

closing them without investigation—is a problematic solution to budget and resources woes.

"If they don't continue to dump cases, Congress will say, 'Well, what did you do with the money we gave you?'" Martin said. But they can't make the case for more funding, she said, if they appear to be succeeding without it ... Eleanor Holmes Norton, who headed the agency from 1977 to 1981, is one of the few members of Congress who have consistently pushed to bolster [strengthen] protections for employment discrimination. But as the representative for Washington, DC, she has no vote. Her perspective: Most lawmakers have little interest in fighting discrimination ... Labor economist William Spriggs isn't surprised by ... the funding constraints that affect workers' chances of help at the EEOC. Congress's treatment of employment discrimination and workers' rights, he said, is par for the course in the U.S.

"There is a tendency in society to think of labor law as littering or something," he said. "They don't think of it as an actual violation."[1]

1. Maryam Jameel, "More and More Workplace Discrimination Cases Are Being Closed Before They're Even Investigated," Vox, June 14, 2019, www.vox.com/identities/2019/6/14/18663296/congress-eeoc-workplace-discrimination.

compared with white families, who earn on average $120,000. Other racial groups were not included in the study.

Although companies often try to be diverse, people of color rarely fill leadership roles in the United States. In 2016, there were only five black chief executive officers (CEOs) in America's 500 biggest companies, known as Fortune 500 companies. Only one black woman has ever held such a position—Ursula Burns, who was the CEO of Xerox until 2016. When Burns and Kenneth Chenault, CEO of American Express, stepped down from their positions, they were replaced with white men, bringing the total number of black CEOs in Fortune 500 companies down to three as of 2018. David A. Thomas, a professor at Harvard Business School, said, "People of color who start at the same time as an equivalent white person have less of a chance of being at the top echelon [level] in 20 years, in whatever field you're talking about."[5] Seeing role models that a person can relate to is one thing that has been known to boost career opportunities. Without people of color in leadership roles, many see a bleak future in which this lack of opportunity will surely persist.

Racial discrimination also occurs early in the employment process, as a 2003 study showed. Researchers Marianne Bertrand of the University of Chicago and Dean Karlan of Yale University sent out nearly 5,000 fictional résumés in Boston, Massachusetts, and Chicago, Illinois. These résumés were randomly assigned either "white-sounding" names, such as Emily and Greg, or "black-sounding" names, such as Lakisha and Jamal. Bertrand and Karlan discovered that the résumés with white-sounding names received 50 percent more calls for interviews than those with black-sounding names, indicating a racial prejudice in hiring practices.

People of color who do get hired may be subjected to unfair practices in the workplace. One example of this was a class action lawsuit against New York City's Parks and Recreation Department. For years, people of color who worked in the department rarely received pay raises comparable with their white counterparts and were typically turned down for promotions. Banding together, the employees sued the city, and after nine years, they won their court battle. The 2008 settlement awarded the workers $21 million, much of it in back pay, and the department agreed to change its policies and procedures to ensure fairness in the future.

Discrimination in Schools

The workplace is only one area in which racism and prejudice frequently appear. In schools, various forms of racism and racial insensitivity challenge teachers and students around the world on a regular basis. For example, during Trump's presidential campaign and presidency, instances were reported of students chanting "Build the wall" at nonwhite students—a reference to Trump's proposed border wall between the United States and Mexico. On its website, CNN posted a video of one such incident as well as people's reactions to it.

One big problem students of color face is unequal discipline in the classroom. According to the American Civil Liberties Union (ACLU), black students make up 15 percent of students in American public schools, but they made up 31 percent of the students who were arrested or reported to law enforcement during the 2015–2016 school year. The Department of Education's Office of Civil Rights (OCR) noted that this isn't because black students behave worse than white students. Instead, it has to do with teachers' bias.

One issue that's rarely talked about by major media outlets is known as the "school-to-prison" pipeline. This disproportionately affects students of color. According to the ACLU, "'Zero-tolerance' policies criminalize minor infractions of school rules, while cops in schools lead to students being criminalized for behavior that should be handled inside the school."[6] The ACLU noted that a big reason for this is that many public schools are underfunded and overcrowded. When teachers have few resources available to them, they become overwhelmed and are less able to help individual students. Lack of funding also means there are no school counselors and no special education classes, increasing the risk of students acting out in class—and being referred to law enforcement—or dropping out of school completely, which can sometimes lead to criminal activity that lands a former student in prison.

The idea behind zero-tolerance policies is generally safety. Schools have rules against bringing in weapons, for obvious reasons. However, some schools have classified things such as nail clippers and scissors as weapons, leading students to be expelled or suspended for having them. The ACLU noted, "Suspended and expelled children are often left unsupervised and without constructive activities; they also can easily fall behind in their coursework, leading to a greater likelihood of disengagement and drop-outs. All of these factors increase the likelihood of court involvement."[7] Some schools also rely on police to keep order in the hallways, which has led to an increase in school-based arrests for nonviolent behavior.

Some schools have hired police officers to keep order. This has led to an increase in students—especially black students—being arrested at school.

Students of color are far more likely to be targeted this way, even when they aren't being any more disruptive than their white peers.

Black students are also more likely to be targeted by the school for punishments regarding dress codes. For example, students have been sent home from school for things such as wearing their hair in dreadlocks. A dress code policy that specifically forbids hairstyles that are almost exclusively worn by black students not only falsely implies that the students aren't appropriate, clean, or safe, it also hurts their education by taking them out of class for something that doesn't negatively affect them or other students.

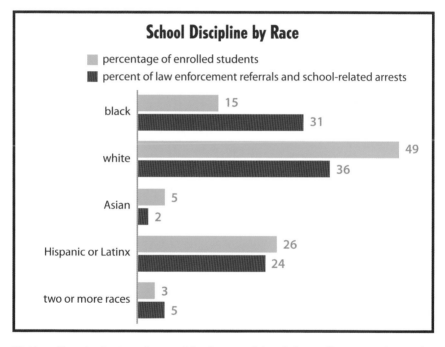

School Discipline by Race

percentage of enrolled students

percent of law enforcement referrals and school-related arrests

black: 15 / 31
white: 49 / 36
Asian: 5 / 2
Hispanic or Latinx: 26 / 24
two or more races: 3 / 5

Nationally, students who are black or multiracial are disproportionately arrested or referred to law enforcenement, as this information from the US Department of Education Office for Civil Rights shows.

Race also plays a part in which students are able to advance to higher education. In 2019, the American Council on Education released a report on the state of education in the United States. One of its findings was that graduation rates increased for all races between 2013 and 2016. Black students saw the most growth, going from about 71 percent to about 76 percent. Native American high schoolers are the most disadvantaged race in the United States; their graduation rate is only about 72 percent, up from about 70 percent in 2013. Sociologists don't believe that racism is the sole cause for this lack of achievement, but it may be one key factor, especially because race has been shown to affect other factors, such as poverty rates. In cities and on reservations, crumbling buildings, outdated textbooks, and unqualified staff discourage students from staying in school. Even for students who aren't arrested or expelled, financial pressures force thousands of students into the workforce before completing their high school education.

Those who do graduate and attend college are better off but still face problems. *The Atlantic* reported that black people with a college degree still face unemployment at greater rates than white people—their unemployment rate is almost equal to white people with only a high school degree. Black college graduates also face twice as many student loans as white college graduates, so they start off at an economic disadvantage.

Microaggressions

Racism exists in many forms. Sometimes it's very obvious, as with racially motivated hate crimes, and sometimes it's subtle, such as a racially insensitive comment. Regardless of the form racism takes, it's always damaging. Racist comments, even accidental ones, give the impression that people of color are somehow inferior to whites.

Many people say or do things to people of color that are considered offensive simply because these people don't consider how their actions will make the other person feel. Other times, people are intentionally offensive. One type of racist comment or action is called a microaggression. Microaggressions are "brief and commonplace daily verbal, behavioral, or environmental indignities, whether intentional or unintentional, that communicate hostile, derogatory, or negative racial slights and insults toward people of color."[8] Microaggressions are often different for different races.

For Native Americans, it may be questions such as, "Do you live in a tipi?," or the assumption that they abuse alcohol. For East Asians, it may be remarks such as, "What country did you come from?," which assumes that the person was born in Asia, when in fact many people of Asian descent are born and raised in the country they currently live in. Many people also don't take the time to find out which Asian country a person is from and tend to assume that all Asian people are Chinese. Black people may face comments such as, "You're pretty for a black girl," "You don't act like a regular black person," or "You're very well-spoken," which assumes that there's one particular type of black person and that anyone who breaks this mold is better. They may also have to answer questions that are differently worded than questions that are asked of white people. For instance, while a white woman may be asked, "Do you have any kids?," a black woman may be asked, "How many kids do you have?"

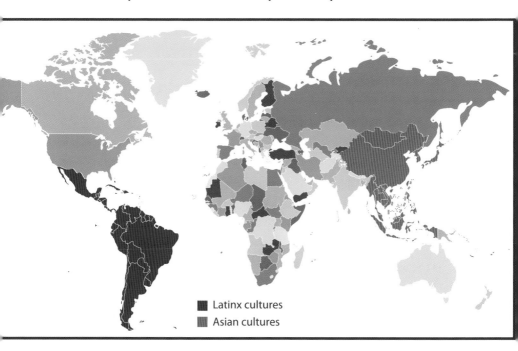

Latinx cultures
Asian cultures

Americans tend to think that all Latinx people are Mexican and all East Asians—as well as some Southeast Asians, such as Vietnamese and Thai people—are Chinese. In reality, Latinx and Asian people come from dozens of different countries, including those highlighted on this map.

Arab and Middle Eastern people may be asked if they are Muslim or terrorists. Latinx people may receive comments about how they must love tacos, and many tend to assume all Latinx are Mexican. Biracial or multiracial people who appear white may be told that they're not actually people of color. Anyone who doesn't appear white may be complimented on their English, which assumes that they weren't raised in an English-speaking country.

These are only a few of the numerous microaggressions people of all races hear on a daily basis. Some can be directed at any race, while others are specific to one race. People who commit microaggressions often don't do so on purpose and may not see anything wrong with what they said. However, when microaggressions are experienced on a daily basis, they can be very damaging, giving people of color the impression that they're outsiders in their own country. It may not seem like a big deal to ask a Latinx person if they like tacos or a black person if they like fried chicken, but these microaggressions assume that food preferences are based on genetics and disregard the fact that many people, regardless of skin color, enjoy these foods.

Sometimes people say things without thinking or make a genuine mistake that comes off as racist. In that case, it's still extremely important to respect the other person's feelings. If a person of color tells a white person, "That remark was racist and I feel offended," the white person should not try to explain themselves by saying things such as, "It was a joke," "Here's why I said that," or "You're too sensitive." Instead, they should recognize that they accidentally hurt someone's feelings and simply say, "I'm sorry, I didn't realize. I'll remember that in the future."

Noticing Privilege

Sometimes racism can be so subtle that a person may not even be aware of their own prejudices. However, in most spheres of American life, race remains a powerful, if often unspoken, fact of life. Part of the reason racism is sometimes tolerated may be that white people often find it difficult to recognize that they have privilege. There are thousands of ways white people benefit from the color of their

Does Reverse Racism Exist?

When white people are insulted by a person of color or excluded from certain things that are centered around people of color, they sometimes say they've experienced reverse racism—racism against white people by people of color. They may cite the fact that there is a Black History Month but no White History Month, or claim that the BLM movement spreads the idea that white people's lives don't matter. If they are called a racial slur by a person of color, they may also say they have experienced reverse racism. However, reverse racism doesn't exist.

Prejudice is a dislike of a person or group based on the idea that all members of that group have the same characteristics; for instance, a black person who assumes that all white people are snobby has a prejudice against white people. However, racism is a social system that disadvantages people of any nonwhite race. White people "do not face housing or job discrimination, police brutality, poverty, or incarceration [jail time] at the level that [people of color] do. That is not to say that they do not experience things like poverty and police brutality at all. But again, *not on the same scale*—not even close. *That* is the reality of racism."[1] Since white people have more privilege in places such as the United States and Europe, they still benefit from the social system even if they experience prejudice from a person of color. This is why Black History Month and BLM are not racist: Society assumes by default that white lives matter and that every month is White History Month.

1. Zeba Blay, "4 'Reverse Racism' Myths That Need to Stop," *HuffPost*, modified June 6, 2017, www.huffpost.com/entry/reverse-racism-isnt-a-thing_n_55d60a91e4b07addcb45da97.

skin, ranging from minor—for example, seeing more white people than people of color in movies—to major—for instance, not having to worry that any encounter with the police may turn violent. White people tend to get defensive when asked to think about the ways their privilege benefits them; they often believe people of color are too sensitive to racial slights and that when people tell them they have privilege, they are implying that white people don't ever have to work hard. This is untrue; many white people work hard to achieve success. A white musician who practices several hours a day, a white student who studies to pass every test, and a white job candidate who spends time finding internships and writing a strong cover letter are all hard workers. However, people of color often have to work harder than white people to achieve the same

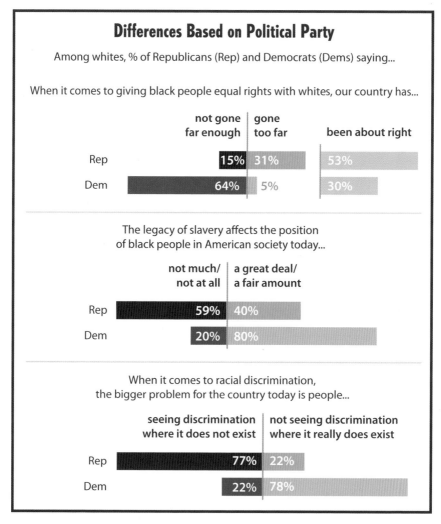

Differences Based on Political Party

Among whites, % of Republicans (Rep) and Democrats (Dems) saying...

When it comes to giving black people equal rights with whites, our country has...

	not gone far enough	gone too far	been about right
Rep	15%	31%	53%
Dem	64%	5%	30%

The legacy of slavery affects the position of black people in American society today...

	not much/ not at all	a great deal/ a fair amount
Rep	59%	40%
Dem	20%	80%

When it comes to racial discrimination, the bigger problem for the country today is people...

	seeing discrimination where it does not exist	not seeing discrimination where it really does exist
Rep	77%	22%
Dem	22%	78%

A person's political views and their views on racism are often related, as this information from the Pew Research Center shows.

successes. White privilege simply means that, although a white person may have faced disadvantages in their life, the color of their skin isn't one of them.

As Molefi Kete Asante explained in *Erasing Racism: The Survival of the American Nation*, racial discrimination persists in society in both overt and subtle ways. Asante wrote:

> We [black people] walk into an automobile showroom and we are quoted higher prices than whites; we work as cooks in restaurants where whites with less skill and less time in the job are paid more; we step into employment agencies and they direct us away from jobs, high school counselors direct us away from African American Studies courses where we can learn about our history and culture. We are told that there are no apartments available, but when our white friends call the same agency they are told there are several apartments available.[9]

White people often become upset when people of color try to create clubs or groups specifically for them. White people tend to claim that such groups do more to promote racism than erase it because people of color are setting themselves apart and pointing out their own race, rather than trying to assimilate with white culture so that race is no longer an issue. However, these arguments suggest that white people would rather make race disappear than talk about it. They may speak of not wanting to have it "shoved in their faces," forgetting that for people of color, white culture is all around them all the time. Additionally, this view doesn't take into account the fact that people of color often need these groups to connect with people who have shared values and experiences in a place where they feel safe.

In 2015, a group called POC Yoga offered yoga classes for people of color (POC) of all ages, genders, sexual orientations, and abilities. The group respectfully asked white people not to attend. After POC Yoga was criticized and called racist by a talk show host for excluding white people, one of the founders of the group, Teresa Wang, received hundreds of angry emails, phone calls, and death threats from white people. According to Joe R. Feagin, a

What's Intersectionality?

Because issues such as race, gender, sexuality, and class are so complex, people tend to discuss one at a time. However, in real life, all of these issues influence each other. This influence is known as intersectionality, and it means that because people of color, women, members of the LGBTQ+ community, people who live in poverty, and other groups all experience disadvantage, a poor Latina woman will experience more disadvantage than a wealthy Latina woman, a poor white woman, or a poor Latino man.

It's sometimes difficult for people to remember intersectionality, so exclusion sometimes happens even within social justice movements. For instance, the Women's March on Washington in January 2017 was originally organized completely by white women. After receiving criticism for this, they made an effort to include women of color. According to Ruth Enid Zambrana, director of the Consortium on Race, Gender and Ethnicity at the University of Maryland, "White women need to recognize that gender isn't a single category. There is a need to acknowledge underrepresented women and domestic groups that have different histories and are at a tremendous disadvantage."[1]

1. Quoted in Alia E. Dastagir, "What Is Intersectional Feminism? A Look at the Term You May Be Hearing a Lot," *USA Today*, January 19, 2017, www.usatoday.com/story/news/2017/01/19/feminism-intersectionality-racism-sexism-class/96633750.

sociology professor at Texas A&M University, "Those death threats alone illustrate exactly why people of color need safe spaces ... Racism is still extraordinarily widespread in this country and does great harm to people of color ... therefore it is not only logical but necessary that people of color create safe spaces away from whites in which to deal with the stresses of racism and build up strategies to resist."[10]

It may never be possible to completely eliminate racism from society, but in order to at least reduce it, it's necessary for white people to listen to the voices of people of color and try to understand their point of view.

Your Opinion Matters!

1. Have you experienced racism in your own life? Explain your answer.

2. Describe some microaggressions different groups might encounter, and discuss how they can be avoided.

3. What are some ways intersectionality can be applied in everyday life?

WHAT CAUSES RACISM?

There often isn't one single cause of racism. Instead, the causes are wide-ranging and complex. Some people don't even realize they have racist biases, which makes it hard for them to examine and deal with them. Other people know they have racist views but think they're justified. For example, white supremacists are people who have a strong belief that whites are better than other races.

Many racist beliefs are born out of fear and ignorance, and facing those beliefs is often an uncomfortable experience. Even people who support racial justice and equality often have prejudices they don't know about until they suddenly encounter a situation they have never faced before. Racism is perpetuated, or continued, by people who aren't willing to deal with the discomfort of facing their prejudices.

Afraid of Differences

Racism begins with the idea that humans can be separated into different groups based on perceived physical differences, such as skin color, facial features, and hair texture. These differences are the basis for what is commonly thought of as "race." Years ago, it was believed that people with different features were genetically different from one another.

◀ White supremacy is often portrayed as "saving" or "defending" white people. However, racial equality is not a threat to white people.

Today, with advances in the study of human genetics, scientists now know that people of different races are not biologically separate. In fact, human beings, no matter where they're from or what their perceived race is, are generally the same in their genetic makeup. Race is merely a social construct.

Even so, people continue to separate others into distinct "races" and form ideas and opinions about what each race is like. This is due in part to the human tendency to form stereotypes, or oversimplified ways of categorizing other people. The need for a way to put various people into general groups most likely arose in the earliest days of human existence, when knowing which group, family, or tribe one belonged to was necessary for survival. Stereotypes may provide people with a shorthand way to categorize others, but they can be very harmful. They can lead to the belief that because certain people are classified as a group, they must all be alike. This is especially harmful when a stereotype involves negative traits being associated with a group. For example, various groups of people throughout history have been viewed as dishonest, lazy, unintelligent, violent, and many other negative attributes. The belief that whole groups of people hold undesirable traits can lead to racial prejudice—an unfavorable judgment about other people based on the color of their skin.

Stereotypes and racial prejudice can lead to a mistrust of people from another racial group. This happens more frequently when people don't have a chance to really get to know someone of a different race—a common occurrence when neighborhoods, schools, clubs, and other social arenas aren't often racially mixed. People tend to gravitate socially to others who are like them. This means they may have few chances to see firsthand that many of the racial stereotypes they've learned from other people aren't true.

The American Psychological Association (APA) points out that it's human nature for people to avoid things that make them feel anxious or uncomfortable. This avoidance contributes to many people's lack of experience with people of another race, which can, in turn, reinforce negative stereotypes and lead to inaccurate assumptions about anyone who is a different race. These

Religion and Racism

Sometimes people confuse race and religion because so many people of a particular race also follow a particular religion. The two religions this occurs with most commonly are Judaism and Islam. Anti-Semitism is the term for prejudice against Jews, while Islamophobia is the similar term for prejudice against Muslims. Judaism and Islam are religions that anyone of any race can convert to, but they're most often practiced by people who share a common heritage. People who may not belong to either of these religions but appear to have the same features as someone who does may also be discriminated against. Sociologist Stuart Hall called this cultural racism, which "happens when certain people perceive their beliefs and customs as being culturally superior to the beliefs and customs of other groups of people."[1] Since race is a concept that was made up by society, it's technically possible for the definition of race to shift over time. However, as of 2020, race is still used mainly to separate people based on skin color and other physical features.

1. Craig Considine, "Muslims Aren't a Race, So I Can't Be Racist, Right? Wrong," *HuffPost*, modified November 19, 2015, www.huffpost.com/entry/muslims-are-not-a-race_b_8591660.

assumptions may then lead to fear that somehow a person's life will be negatively impacted by a racial group. This fear and mistrust of others goes hand in hand with prejudice and can lead to a person developing negative and hostile attitudes toward others based solely on their race. Such attitudes can also lead to a belief that one race is naturally "better" than another.

Feeling Better Than Others

Racial prejudice often develops from one race's sense of superiority over another. When the first colonists came to what is now the United States, they believed the land they encountered belonged to them simply because they had landed there. They viewed the

Native Americans who were living there as savages because they lived in different types of shelters, had different customs, and wore different clothing than the Europeans. In the early United States, the belief that black people were an inferior race was the cornerstone of slavery. Even after slavery ended, generations of prejudice encouraged white people to view themselves as better than black people.

Many white people also have a bias against people from other countries. It's a common belief that immigrants, especially those who come to the United States illegally, keep white Americans unemployed by taking jobs that would otherwise have gone to them. However, studies have shown that immigrants and

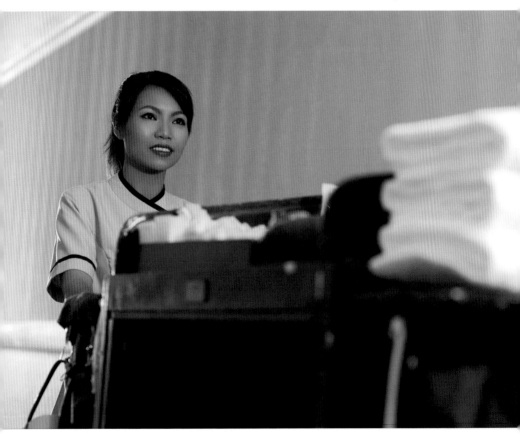

Many immigrants find work as hotel housekeepers—a job few native-born Americans want.

native-born Americans don't compete for the same jobs, even when they have similar levels of education. Immigrants without high school degrees tend to hold jobs such as agricultural worker, house cleaner, and cook, while native-born workers without high school degrees tend to hold jobs such as janitor or building cleaner, truck driver, and cashier.

People who don't speak English well or speak it with an accent are also often looked down on by fluent English speakers because they automatically assume someone who doesn't speak their language well isn't as intelligent as they are. The TV show *Modern Family* pointed out this bias in a scene where the character Gloria, who is from Colombia, has an argument with her husband. She says, "Do you know how frustrating it is to have to translate everything in my head before I say it? To have people laugh in my face because I'm struggling to find the words? You should try talking in my shoes for one mile." When her husband says, "I think you meant …" Gloria responds, "I know what I meant to mean. Do you know how smart I am in Spanish? Of course you don't."[1]

People of color have historically had little political and cultural power in the United States. They were typically kept in second-class status and had no access to the kinds of education available to most whites. Although the laws of the country state that race is not a barrier to running for political office, people of color are less likely to be elected because of the attitude of white superiority that still exists in the United States and other countries, at both a conscious and unconscious level.

Part of the reason this attitude of white superiority continues to exist is that it allows white people to feel good about their own identity and that of their group. Being part of the dominant group in a society—or the "in" group—can lead some people to believe that they actually are superior in some way to members of the "out" group. In addition, members of the "in" group enjoy certain benefits and advantages. The APA explained why prejudices and stereotypes that give privilege to one group over another often remain unexamined:

Because stereotypes may help us feel better about ourselves, we avoid challenging these stereotypes. In other words, we become defensive and protective of our worldviews and only reluctantly question our deepest assumptions. And these worldviews help protect not only our self-esteem, but also real-world privileges and benefits that accrue [add up] to us as members of an in group. For example, racist discrimination by banks that hurts African American communities by limiting mortgages to these areas also benefits White neighborhoods by making more money available to them ... So, maintaining our prejudiced views of others allows us to feel better about our own group and to avoid challenging unfair social practices that benefit us.[2]

Keeping these negative racist ideas and prejudicial attitudes intact enables white people to maintain the power and advantages they hold in society. This is known as "white privilege." Some people—for example, members of white supremacy groups—are very aware of their desire to keep white privilege intact. Others may never have stopped to think about the fact that they enjoy certain advantages simply because they're white. However, whether people acknowledge it or not, white privilege remains a factor in interactions between people of color and white people today. When white people refuse to acknowledge their privilege, they tend to look down on people of color who haven't had the same advantages. This can lead people who believe they aren't racist to hold racist views, such as thinking that black people have a more difficult time achieving success because they don't work as hard as white people.

Racial Profiling and Police Brutality

Racial profiling is a method of using racial or ethnic characteristics to determine whether a person is likely to commit a crime. Law enforcement agencies around the world have relied on racial profiling for years to predict who will or will not commit a crime. For example, since the terrorist attacks on the United States on September 11, 2001, fears of more attacks have led to greater

A controversial policy called stop-and-frisk, which says police can stop and search anyone they suspect of committing a crime, became a major part of law enforcement in New York City around 2002. Research found that black and Latinx people were nine times more likely to be targeted, even if police had no reason to suspect them of anything.

security screening of Arab and Middle Eastern people as well as those with a similar skin tone, such as people from Southeast Asia. These people are stopped, searched, and sometimes barred from boarding airplanes.

Millions of people of color experience racial profiling on a daily basis. Security officials charged with protecting citizens argue that these tactics are necessary, but studies have shown they aren't effective in finding criminals. Critics say they're also unfair and that racial profiling leads to further racial prejudice because it reinforces the negative stereotype of certain people of color as untrustworthy, which contributes to such attitudes permeating society.

In 2017, after Donald Trump ordered an immigration ban on people traveling from a number of Muslim-majority countries, a brown-skinned United States citizen named Aravinda Pillalamarri was stopped by police while she was out for a walk in her neighborhood in Bel Air, Maryland. The police said someone who lived in the neighborhood had reported her as a suspicious person. "I had just come out for a walk, so I didn't have my ID. And he said, 'Why don't you have ID? Are you here illegally?'" she told reporters. The Bel Air police denied that it was a case of racial profiling, saying, "They were trying to figure out why there was some hesitation to provide identification … That's why he asked if she was illegal."[3] However, critics pointed out that police would be unlikely to ask a white person the same question.

The racial profiling of black drivers has become so common in the United States that a phrase has been invented to describe it. "Driving While Black," or DWB, may be a symptom of deepseated racial prejudice. The fact that it happens so often may also contribute to society's negative perceptions of black people. In other words, people assume that black people must be criminals or bad drivers because of how often they get pulled over, even though many times they haven't done anything to deserve getting pulled over.

Sometimes a police encounter that would be routine for a white person turns dangerous or deadly for a person of color. In 2016, a 32-year-old black man named Philando Castile was shot by Minnesota police after they stopped him because his taillight

Measuring Unknown Bias

People often respond to one another based on attitudes they hold about each other's race—attitudes they may hold at an unconscious level. In fact, one of the main motivations for racial prejudice may actually be deeply ingrained racist attitudes that people are unaware they hold.

The Implicit Association Test (IAT) is designed to measure the speed with which people categorize images and words they are shown. There are several types of IATs that measure bias in various areas, such as gender, age, and race. Malcolm Gladwell, who has a white father and a black mother, wrote extensively about IATs in his book, *Blink*. After taking the test himself, he felt slightly embarrassed by his own results. Even though he is well educated and biracial, he, too, discovered he had prejudices he was not even aware of. After taking the test four times, Gladwell was rated as having a "moderate automatic preference for whites."[1] This suggests that attitudes on race are based on both the biases people are aware of and those that are unconscious, or hidden, even from themselves.

However, in 2017, Vox reported that the Harvard researchers who created the IAT were starting to find that the test wasn't very accurate if it was only taken once. They still believe it can be useful if it's taken multiple times and the results are averaged out, but no researcher recommends taking the results of a single test as the ultimate truth of a person's biases.

1. Quoted in Malcolm Gladwell, *Blink: The Power of Thinking Without Thinking* (New York, NY: Little, Brown, 2005), p. 143.

was broken. The officer asked Castile to show his identification, and when Castile reached for his wallet, the officer shot him, assuming that he was reaching for a gun. Mark Dayton, the governor of Minnesota "said he found both the shooting and the aftermath 'absolutely appalling at all levels,' noting in particular that no first aid was provided to Castile, while other police officers did attend to the officer who fired the shots."[4] This is only one of hundreds of incidents of police brutality that have been in the news for the past several years. In response to such tragedies, the group Black Lives Matter organized to fight for racial justice.

The Cycle of Poverty

Because racism makes it harder for people of color to get certain jobs, many are stuck in a cycle of poverty. Being poor makes it difficult to save money because there are so many things people must pay for on a regular basis just to survive, including food, gas or bus fare to get to work, clothing, shoes, rent, and utilities (heating and water bills). Any large unexpected expenses, such as medical bills, can drive already impoverished people into deep debt. Many people unfairly look down on others who have less prestigious jobs, earn less money, drive less expensive cars, or live in smaller homes than they do. This can be a powerful factor for racism when so many people of color live in poverty. According to the Kaiser Family Foundation, 13 percent of Americans lived below the national poverty threshold in 2018. The US Census Bureau sets the federal poverty level at $20,212 per year for a family of two adults and one child, but states and cities have their own poverty levels as well; for instance, $20,000 will take a family much farther in Lincoln, Nebraska, than it will in New York City.

People of color are disproportionately impoverished. Of the 13 percent of Americans living in poverty, 22 percent were black, 19 percent were Hispanic, 11 percent were Asian, and 24 percent were Native American. Only 9 percent were whites. Although poverty is difficult no matter what race someone is, it's undeniable that people of color are more likely to live in poverty than white people. For those who are born in the United States, a big part of the problem is intergenerational poverty. This means that if someone's parents are poor, that person is also likely to be poor because their parents have less opportunity to give them certain advantages. For example, a person who grows up in a poor family may have use money from their part-time job to help contribute to the household. In contrast, a person whose parents make enough money to support the whole family can keep all the money they make at their job. Even if they both get jobs at the same age, the wealthier person will have more money saved up a year later than the poorer person. Education is also a factor. Someone who has to drop out of high school to help support their family or who is kicked out of school for racially motivated reasons has less opportunity to get a high-paying job than someone who finishes high school.

People of color who come to the United States from other countries also generally have less money and fewer choices when it comes to jobs than American citizens. In 2018, *USA Today* reported that although noncitizen immigrants account for only about 7 percent of the US population, more than 20 percent of them live in poverty.

Native Americans are more likely to live in poverty than any other race, mainly as a result of government policies that have been directed against them since the first white colonists arrived in what is now the United States. On reservations, their land is owned and managed by the federal government, which means they aren't able to make their own economic decisions. The process for approval for projects to improve the economy is often slow; according to *Forbes*, "On Indian lands, companies must go through at least four federal agencies and 49 steps to acquire a permit for energy development. Off reservation, it takes only four steps. This bureaucracy prevents tribes from capitalizing on their resources."[5] The government also controls payments that are made to reservations and sometimes doesn't pay them everything they're owed. This means Native Americans have less money to use for their schools and other public institutions.

To add insult to injury, people of color are sometimes blamed for their own predicament. This is known as victim-blaming, and it generally happens because humans like to believe the world is fair and that bad things only happen to those who deserve it. The thinking goes that if the world is fair, then those who are in a bad situation must have done something to deserve their misfortune. Many people also uphold the unrealistic the idea that if people just tried hard enough, they could make their

Due in large part to unfair federal policies, Native Americans who live on reservations are more likely to experience poverty.

situation better. Partially, this way of thinking happens because white people who have had more advantages don't always recognize their privilege. They may say they've struggled but overcome the odds, and therefore others can too. This mindset plays a part in racist attitudes; many assume that people of color are poor because they're lazy or don't care enough about their situation to do something about it. In reality, the vast majority of people who live in poverty work extremely hard, often holding two or more jobs just to make ends meet. Victim-blaming is something that is deeply ingrained in society, and many people may not realize they hold such an attitude.

Knowing that many people of color live in poverty can sometimes lead people to assume that all people of color live in poverty. Sometimes this leads to discrimination, such as refusing to serve a person of color in a store based on the assumption that the person doesn't have money to pay for what they're looking at. Other times, it leads people to say or do offensive things that they believe are nice or helpful, such as telling a person of color where the nearest soup kitchen is or offering to buy them a meal. This is rude and offensive because it assumes that any person of color must be homeless or poor, when in reality, many people of color overcome the odds that are stacked against them to achieve high status and wealth.

For Asians—especially East Asians—unlike many other people of color, the stereotypes are generally positive. In the past, they were highly discriminated against with policies such as the Chinese Exclusion Act, which banned Chinese immigrants from 1882 to 1943, as well as the forced internment of Japanese-American citizens after the Japanese attack on Pearl Harbor in 1941. Over time, perceptions changed, and today, Asians are generally seen as hardworking, intelligent, and successful. However, this doesn't mean they don't suffer from racism; they do still encounter harmful stereotypes and daily microaggressions, such as comments about their facial features, insults about their various cultures, and subtle expectations that they constantly prove how American they are. Additionally, according to Josh Ishimatsu, deputy director of the National Coalition for Asian Pacific American Community Development, "There's a presumption that all [Asian-Americans and Pacific Islanders] are rich and educated ... The people who are not don't have much in the way of services available—they're just not known or seen."[6]

Being seen as high-achieving can make it difficult for Asians—including East Asians from China, Japan, and Korea, as well as Southeast Asians from places such as India, Cambodia, Pakistan, and the Philippines—to get access to the services they need when they live in poverty or to be taken seriously when they speak about the problems they face. White people also may not see stereotypes of Asians as racist because the associations are generally

After the bombing of Pearl Harbor in 1941, Americans of Japanese descent were targeted out of fear that they would be more loyal to Japan than to the United States. Many had most of their money and property taken away and were forcibly relocated to internment camps.

positive rather than negative, which makes it difficult to make people see that they need to change their perceptions.

Asians may be seen publicly as a "model minority," but sometimes world events uncover the hidden biases many people around the world have against them. In early 2020, an outbreak of a type of coronavirus experts called COVID-19—but which many people simply called "the coronavirus" or even just "corona"—started spreading around the world. The virus originated in Wuhan, China, and panic over the outbreak brought people's ingrained racism to the forefront. Some news commentators spread false rumors they picked up from social media that the virus had been caused by Chinese people eating bats or other live animals, which caused many people to accuse the Chinese of being disgusting, uncivilized, or dirty. Long before the first outbreak in the United States, Americans started going out of their way to avoid Chinese restaurants and any Asian person they perceived to be Chinese, despite the fact that the virus isn't genetic and can be passed on by any infected person of any race. Some people even called for all Chinese people, whether they were infected or not, to be deported from the United States. These racist reactions show how quickly people turn on anyone who is seen as different.

The reasons for racism are varied and complex. Some are centuries old, while others have come about more recently. Many stem from unconscious attitudes that people hold and never think about. However, racism is embedded in society, even at the unconscious level.

Your Opinion Matters!

1. What are some of the ways in which stereotypes can be harmful to people?
2. How can you fight discrimination in your school?
3. What biases do you hold? How can you overcome them?

RESISTANCE TO CHANGE

In the United States today, there are laws in place that are meant to promote racial justice. These include laws that prevent someone from refusing to rent an apartment to a person of color, refusing to serve them at a restaurant, or committing a hate crime against them. Some of these laws are controversial, and people have campaigned to have them repealed.

Although passing laws against racist actions is a good thing, it's not the whole solution because laws don't change people's attitudes. Some of the laws are easy to get around. Additionally, some things aren't illegal but are still racist and can have a damaging effect on people of color. Since white people are seen as the majority in Western society, beauty products, dolls, movies, advertisements, and many other aspects of Western culture are aimed at them. This often sends a message to people of color that they aren't as important as white people. Many white people—even those with good intentions—are so used to seeing these things that they've stopped noticing how common they are until the imbalance is pointed out to them.

Claiming Another's Culture

Cultural appropriation "involves members of a dominant group exploiting the culture of less privileged groups. Quite often, this

◀ It can be hard for people of color to find dolls that match their skin tone.

is done along racial and ethnic lines with little understanding of the latter's history, experience, and traditions."[1] This may include hairstyles, clothing, musical styles, or other aspects of a particular culture. Exchange of cultural ideas has taken place for centuries and isn't always a bad thing. Sometimes it broadens people's horizons and introduces them to new, interesting things. However, it turns into cultural appropriation when the group in power profits from the cultures of minority groups—often while preventing people in those groups from profiting themselves. For example, Urban Outfitters has come under fire for selling Native American-inspired clothing and jewelry because actual Native Americans aren't involved in the process and because often, people buy from Urban Outfitters rather than from Native American sellers. Another form of cultural appropriation is when a person who doesn't belong to a cultural group uses that culture in ways that are offensive. Even people who aren't white can be guilty of such actions.

One example of cultural appropriation that has sparked much controversy is when people wear Native American headdresses and face paint that's meant to imitate Native American war paint—two practices that are especially common at music festivals. Many people wear them because they like the way they look, but Native Americans have made it clear that this practice is offensive for a number of reasons. According to the website Native Appropriations, one is that people who aren't Native American are pretending to be, which is similar to blackface—the racist practice of putting on black makeup to pretend to be a black person. Another is that warbonnets and feathers have a strong spiritual meaning in many Native American cultures, so when people who have no ties to the culture wear them, it shows a lack of respect for Native Americans and their practices. A third reason is that the picture of a Native American wearing those items

is one that has been created and perpetuated by Hollywood and only bears minimal resemblance to traditional regalia of Plains tribes. It furthers the stereotype that Native peoples are one monolithic culture, when in fact there are 500+ distinct tribes with their own cultures. It also places Native people in the historic past, as something that cannot exist in modern society. We don't walk around in ceremonial attire [every day], but we still exist and are Native.[2]

Some people feel that cultural appropriation isn't a problem because there's so much overlap among different cultures in the modern world; for instance, many non-Japanese people eat sushi, many Westerners find the Eastern practice of meditation calming, and many non-Native Americans think turquoise jewelry is pretty. However, cultural appropriation is a problem "when the new adoption is void of the significance that it was supposed to have—it strips the religious, historical and cultural context of something and makes it mass-marketable."[3] For example, yoga has become controversial. Yoga originated in India as a spiritual practice more than 5,000 years ago, but in the 21st century, it's become a common way for Westerners to both relax and exercise. Many people agree that there's nothing wrong with liking yoga; it's the way it's often

Some people sell "Native-inspired" jewelry with fake, inexpensive turquoise in it. This has caused consumers to devalue real turquoise, hurting Native American craftsmen who rely on selling their jewelry to make a living.

marketed to white Westerners that's problematic. Using it solely as an exercise class, shaming others who have trouble holding the poses, or ignoring the practice's Indian roots are all ways yoga can be culturally appropriated.

It's important to remember that not all people of color share the same opinions. One person might not be offended by something that someone else is offended by. If someone tells you that they're upset with what you're doing or saying, it's inappropriate to say that you have another friend of the same race who told you that you're allowed to do or say whatever the person is taking issue with.

Understanding Whitewashing

Whitewashing is a term that can refer to several things. One is when a photo of a person of color is edited to look like they have lighter skin than they really do. This happens frequently in beauty magazines: Dark-skinned women who pose for photo shoots are often seen on the covers of magazines such as *Vanity Fair*, *Vogue*, and *Elle* with noticeably lighter skin. The magazines often blame the lighting at the photo shoot for this effect, but people who work in the photo industry have countered that claim by saying that photographers have special equipment that prevents this from happening. In reality, it's more likely that these photographs have been digitally edited to make the women appear to have lighter skin. This is damaging because it contributes to a perception of beauty that is Eurocentric, or focused on the way white European women look. A Eurocentric standard of beauty may cause dark-skinned women to feel that they are less beautiful than women with lighter skin.

Another example can be seen on book covers. Sometimes a book that has a main character of color will have a cover that features a white person, someone who could be seen as white, or someone whose face is hidden. In some cases, publishers have changed their covers in response to outrage from authors and readers. For instance, the book *Liar* by Justine Larbalestier describes the main character, Micah, as a black girl who wears her hair natural. When the book was first released, however, the cover featured a black-and-white photo of a girl who was clearly white, with straight hair. In response

A Diverse Cast

Hamilton: An American Musical is a musical created by Lin-Manuel Miranda, an American playwright and actor of Puerto Rican descent. It premiered off-Broadway in February 2015, but was so popular that it quickly moved to Broadway. Tickets were difficult to get, and available seats could cost more than $900.

One thing that sets *Hamilton* apart from other shows is its diverse cast. The majority of the cast is made up of black or Latinx actors. Some claim this is discrimination against white actors, but most note that this is simply how casting works—the director is allowed to choose the people they think best represent the story being told. The casting call originally specified nonwhite actors, but Actors' Equity, the theater actors' union, said that although the show can specify the race, gender, and age of each character, the auditions must be open to anyone of any race. In response to this criticism, the language of the casting call was changed to reflect the fact that white actors were welcome to try out.

One of Miranda's goals was to give black and Latinx actors a chance to take roles that are traditionally denied to them because of the color of their skin, and in this he succeeded. According to *HuffPost*, the show "is a musical that lives and breathes hip-hop. Its music and diverse cast, juxtaposed with the story of a country just beginning to find its voice, perfectly reflect the complex racial history and identity of America."[1] A movie version featuring the original cast is set to come out on October 15, 2021.

1. Zeba Blay, "No, the 'Hamilton' Casting Call for 'Non-White' Actors is Not Reverse Racism," *HuffPost*, modified November 22, 2016, www.huffpost.com/entry/no-the-hamilton-casting-call-for-non-white-actors-is-not-reverse-racism_n_56fd2c83e4b0daf53aeed9b9.

to backlash by the public, the publishing company changed the cover to show a light-skinned black girl with curly hair.

Another meaning of whitewashing is when a white person is cast as a person of color in a movie or TV show. One example is the 2016 film *Gods of Egypt*. As the title makes clear, the movie was set in Egypt, but the cast was almost entirely white, so it received much criticism. The director and the film company apologized to the public for the choice of casting, but it was too late to change anything. Another example is *Ghost in the Shell*, a 2017 movie starring Scarlett Johansson set in a futuristic Japan. Rupert Sanders, the movie's director, stated that he cast Johansson because she was the best actress for the part, but many people were upset that a white actress was cast as a Japanese character. Some people feel that it doesn't matter who's cast in a movie as long as the acting is good, but whitewashing makes it harder for people of color to get acting roles and contributes to the lack of diversity in popular culture.

Even when actors of color do break into the industry, they often have trouble getting recognized for their work. In 2015 and 2016, the hashtag #OscarsSoWhite began trending on social media, highlighting the fact that for two years in a row, not one single person of color had been nominated for an Academy Award, or Oscar, as a lead or supporting actor. Even though some movies featuring actors of color had been highly praised by critics, the Academy of Motion Picture Arts and Sciences—the organization that nominates actors for awards, often referred to simply as the Academy—had overlooked all of them. In some cases, even when a nominated movie featured people of color, the nomination went to a white person who had worked on the film. For instance, the movie *Straight Outta Compton* starred mainly black people, but its Oscar nomination went to its white screenwriters.

Because of this lack of diversity, many actors and filmmakers chose to boycott the 2016 Oscars. Some people in the industry didn't boycott but did speak out for more diversity in Hollywood. Others dismissed the issue, claiming that the best people were nominated for the awards regardless of race. In response to the outrage, the governing board of the Academy, which was made up primarily of white men, pledged to expand the number of people of color and women in its ranks by 2020. Although they kept this promise, the controversy surfaced again in 2020, when only one actor of color was nominated for an Oscar. Several highly-praised actors were snubbed, including Awkwafina, who was the first Asian American woman in

Awkwafina won a Golden Globe in 2020 for her performance in
The Farewell but wasn't nominated for an Academy Award.

history to win the Golden Globe award for Best Actress in a Motion Picture (Musical or Comedy). This award is often seen as a step on the way to an Oscar nomination, but it was not the case for Awkwafina.

A Controversial Policy

The Academy's promise to diversify its board is one example of affirmative action—a policy of giving special preference to people because of their race, ethnicity, or gender. The goal of affirmative action is to provide equal opportunity and to encourage—even demand—diversity in the workplace, in schools, in government, and in other arenas. Affirmative action can also be implemented to make amends for past wrongs, such as slavery or other racial injustices.

Affirmative action is controversial in the United States. The 14th Amendment to the Constitution, which was ratified in 1868, protects the rights of all American citizens, regardless of race, gender, or religion. People of color, however, continued to be legally discriminated against for another hundred years. In the mid-20th century, white Americans still blatantly received preferential treatment over people of color in virtually all areas of life, including hiring practices, job promotions, wages, housing, and university admissions. The lack of access to a quality education made it even harder for people of color to compete against white people in the workplace. The unemployment rate for black people in the early 1960s was twice that of white people, and black men earned barely more than half of what white men earned. As a consequence, 55 percent of black people were living in poverty in 1960.

President Lyndon B. Johnson was an outspoken champion of civil rights for black people. In a 1965 speech he delivered at Howard University, a predominantly black school in Washington, DC, Johnson explained why he believed that protective measures such as affirmative action were necessary to increase equality. He said in part:

You do not take a person who, for years, has been hobbled by chains and liberate him, bring him up to the starting line of a race and then say, "you are free to compete with all the others," and still justly believe that you have been completely fair. Thus it is not enough just to open the gates of opportunity. All our citizens must have the ability to walk through those gates.[4]

In an effort to combat the racial inequality that existed in the United States, Johnson signed the Civil Rights Act of 1964. This act prohibits discrimination on the basis of race or sex in workplaces, public facilities, unions, and federally funded programs. The act also established the EEOC in 1965, which enforced the use of affirmative action—a policy developed by President John F. Kennedy in 1961. With affirmative action, people of color were to be given preferential treatment in hiring practices and university admissions. Employers were ordered not only to cease discriminating against women and people of color, but also to actively hire them.

Other presidents have amended affirmative action, and dozens of court cases have either challenged or upheld the government policy. Writing in support of affirmative action in 1978, Harry Blackmun, associate justice of the US Supreme Court from 1970 to 1994, said, "In order to get beyond racism, we must first take account of race. There is no other way. And in order to treat some persons equally, we must treat them differently."[5]

Thanks to affirmative action programs, people of color now found themselves being hired for jobs that formerly were closed to them and admitted to universities that formerly barred them. One notable example is Supreme Court justice Clarence Thomas, who attended Yale Law School in the 1970s through the university's affirmative action program. Any organization that accepts more than $50,000 in funding from the government and has 50 or more employees is legally required to develop an affirmative action program. Many people think of this as a quota system, meaning that an organization is legally required to hire a certain number of women or people of color. This has been one of the most controversial aspects of affirmative action; critics call it "reverse discrimination" that unfairly affects white American men who, despite having better qualifications for the job or school, may not be selected because

President John F. Kennedy, shown here, created the affirmative action policy in 1961.

they are not a woman or a person of color. However, these accusations are untrue; quota systems have been banned by the Supreme Court. Legally, race and gender can't be the only basis on which a person is hired or admitted to a school. Instead, affirmative action is a federally mandated policy that requires schools and workplaces to maintain fairness when considering who can be admitted to their organization. For instance, if a college admissions board is looking at two equally qualified candidates but has only one spot left, they can choose to admit the person of color if there's already a low number of people of color at the school. This helps even the playing field between whites and people of color and opens up more opportunities to groups that have historically been discriminated against.

For Asians, affirmative action policies can sometimes be harmful. Because of the belief that they are the "model minority," they are excluded from affirmative action programs but are still often passed over in favor of white candidates. When Asians complain about this unfair treatment, people often blame affirmative action, saying that if black and Latinx people weren't given preferential treatment, Asians would have a better chance. However, this argument overlooks the fact that white people still have the best chance of any race of getting the positions they're seeking.

Some argue that the United States has changed dramatically since affirmative action was first enacted, and therefore the race-based policy is no longer necessary. Instead, they believe affirmative action would serve a better purpose if used to help the economically needy, regardless of race. Some people believed that Barack Obama's election in 2008 proved racism was no longer an issue. However, many people didn't approve of Obama's presidency; some legitimately disagreed with his policies, while others simply disliked him because of the color of his skin. Some consider Trump's election to be retaliation by white people against black people. According to CNN, "Dramatic racial progress in America is inevitably followed by a white backlash, or 'whitelash.' Reconstruction in the 19th century was followed by a century of Jim Crow. The civil rights movement of the 1950s and '60s was followed by President Ronald Reagan and the rise of the religious right."[6] CNN commentator Van Jones, who

People Are Not Mascots

The Washington Redskins are a football team with a controversial name and mascot, which is the face of a Native American man. Their fans defend the name and logo, saying they are intended to honor Native Americans. They also say it's a beloved tradition and that fans would be upset if the name changed. However, critics, including many Native Americans, say the term "redskin" is offensive and often used as a slur. They state that using a person as a sports mascot is offensive as well, since mascots are traditionally objects, animals, or mythological creatures. It's clear that many Native Americans don't view the name and logo as an honor, regardless of how it may have been intended.

Other sports teams that have also received criticism are the Cleveland Indians, the Kansas City Chiefs, the Chicago Blackhawks, and the Atlanta Braves. In 2005, the American Psychological Association (APA) urged all sports teams with Native American names or logos to change them, based on "a growing body of social science literature that shows the harmful effects of racial stereotyping and inaccurate racial portrayals, including the particularly harmful effects of American Indian sports mascots on the social identity development and self-esteem of American Indian young people."[1] As of 2020, professional sports teams have continued to ignore this advice.

1. "Summary of the APA Resolution Recommending Retirement of American Indian Mascots," American Psychological Association, accessed February 14, 2020, www.apa.org/pi/oema/resources/indian-mascots.

used the word whitelash on television after the 2016 election, later clarified that he was speaking specifically about openly racist and white supremacist Trump voters.

White Supremacy in the 21st Century

After the civil rights movement, the United States slowly moved toward a culture that discouraged obvious racism. It became frowned upon for people to use racial slurs or make comments that implied people of color were inferior to whites. However, in private and sometimes in public, many people—most of whom were white—still said these things to others who agreed with their views and complained about what they called PC (politically correct) culture. They wanted to speak freely without being told they were being offensive.

During Trump's campaign, when he also complained about PC culture, a group of his supporters who called themselves the alternative right, or alt-right, became even more vocal. Alt-right members are almost all men and say many things, especially online, that are racist, sexist, and anti-Semitic. When people challenge them, the members of the alt-right accuse their critics of being brainwashed by the liberal media and proclaim that they have the right to free speech in America. Some members of the alt-right have self-identified as Nazis, and most consider themselves white supremacists who believe that the United States should be a "white homeland." Violence has surrounded the movement since it started gaining national attention. On August 11 and 12, 2017, an estimated 600 alt-right members met in Charlottesville, Virginia, for a rally they called Unite the Right. At the rally, they carried lit tiki torches and shouted racist and anti-Semitic chants. On August 12, a woman named Heather Heyer was killed when 20-year-old James Alex Fields Jr. ran his car into a group of people who were protesting against the rally. Two years later, another attendee, who considered himself a white supremacist, was arrested for allegedly threatening violence against a Jewish community center in Youngstown, Ohio. Many other alt-right members have been arrested or jailed for shootings and other violence.

Members of the alt-right see many of Donald Trump's policies—such as his proposed wall on the US–Mexico border and his ban on immigration that targets Muslim-majority countries—as ways of preventing white people from being discriminated against; they see equality with women and people of color as a threat because it would mean losing their privilege. Although equality means that everyone has the same opportunities, the alt-right sees it as a way of giving whites fewer advantages than people of color.

Some people who attended the Unite the Right rally (*shown here*) were dismayed when they were later fired from their jobs or were shunned by friends and relatives. This was a reminder to many that freedom of speech is not the same thing as freedom from consequences.

The alt-right isn't a political party; it's just a group of people with similar views. Although not all members of the alt-right share exactly the same views—for instance, some are anti-Semitic, while others don't have a problem with white Jews—they overwhelmingly believe America would be a better country with less racial diversity. Some interpret Trump's 2016 campaign slogan, "Make America Great Again," to refer to a time in America's past when people of color weren't given a voice and white people were able to do and say whatever they wanted without fear of criticism. In 2018, Vox reported that several people who were running for political office as Republicans shared the alt-right's views, including one man who denied that the Holocaust had ever happened and identified as a Nazi and another who explained on his personal website why he's a white supremacist. Some Republicans have denounced these candidates and stated that they don't represent mainstream Republican views, but the United States is a democracy in which anyone who meets certain requirements can run for office. People who reject these views can ensure that such candidates don't win their elections by voting for someone else.

The alt-right didn't revive racism in the United States; people of color have always experienced racism directed toward them and have fought against it for years. However, the alt-right has brought racism back into the eyes of the white public. Some who previously denied that racism still existed in the United States have begun to see that it is, indeed, still an important social problem. Others still prefer to pretend that the problem doesn't exist because they're uncomfortable with facing their privilege. Being born with privilege doesn't make someone a bad person, but it's important for white people to be able to recognize the privilege they have, use it to be an ally to people of color, and actively join the fight against racism.

Your Opinion Matters!

1. In your opinion, is affirmative action helpful or harmful?
2. Give examples of cultural appropriation and why they're wrong.
3. Why is whitewashing problematic?

FIGHTING AGAINST RACISM

In contrast to past decades, when many people were likely to believe that racism was either decreasing or already gone, people today are more likely to believe that racism is increasing. In 2019, the Pew Research Center reported that 65 percent of poll respondents said that since 2016, they feel it's become more common for people to openly express racist views. Furthermore, 45 percent said they felt it was becoming more acceptable to do so; they felt people weren't being called out for their racism as they might have been in the past. People who identified as Democrats were far more likely than those who identified as Republicans to say that the United States has more work to do in the area of racial justice.

Many white people like the idea of racial justice but aren't sure what they can do to help. They may ask people of color what white people should do, but this puts an unfair burden on people of color. First, one person can't speak for everyone of their race; second, it isn't the responsibility of people of color to explain to white people all the ways in which they're oppressed. This is called emotional labor, and it can be very

◀ In 2019, Disney announced that Halle Bailey would play Ariel in its live-action remake of *The Little Mermaid*. The online backlash to this casting decision showed that many people still feel comfortable openly expressing racist views.

stressful and tiring for someone to do, especially repeatedly or over long periods of time. Instead, it's the job of white people to educate themselves by reading books and articles about how to check their privilege and become better allies. They can also take cues, or hints, from people of color without actually making them do the emotional labor of explaining why something is racist: If someone mentions that a certain thing makes them angry or uncomfortable, a white person can make a mental note not to do it in the future. When mistakes happen, rather than becoming defensive or angry, white people should apologize sincerely and attempt to learn from the situation.

Starting Young

Some people feel that it's inappropriate to teach children about racism, but the truth is that behavior is learned from a young age. Parents are often a child's first teachers. Children's earliest ideas about the way society works, as well as the ways in which people relate to one another, begin within the family setting. Parents and families typically lay the foundation for children's later attitudes toward others. Because of this, a child's ideas about people of other races begin within the home—even if they don't realize it.

Parents are in a unique position to combat racism, and they must be vigilant about challenging racism whenever it appears so that children learn tolerance and respect for others. If parents ignore the issue of racism until their child is older, the child will likely pick up negative opinions from other children, TV, or comments overheard in adult conversation.

Experts agree that all parents should discuss race and acceptance of others with their children. However, a 2019 study by Sesame Workshop, the nonprofit organization behind the TV show *Sesame Street*, revealed a startling statistic. Of the 6,070 families of children ages 3 to 12 in the study, only 10 percent of parents reported speaking about race with their children. Of that 10 percent, 22 percent were black and 6 percent were white. The results of this study mirror those of similar studies done in the past. The author of one such study, Brigitte Vittrup of the

Adults like to think that children don't notice race. In reality, they're constantly getting messages about race from society, including by listening to the adults around them.

Children's Research Lab at the University of Texas, offered one reason why parents may not discuss race openly with their children: Many simply don't feel comfortable doing so.

Reds versus Blues

Some adults may avoid discussing race with their children because they feel that any discussion of race or other characteristics that make another person "different" is impolite. Further, they may fear that discussing race with their children will actually create a racial bias. For years, the commonly held notion was that children wouldn't notice another person's race unless it was pointed out to them. However, as researcher Sean McElwee noted, "Age tells us far less about an individual's likelihood of expressing racist sentiments than factors like education, geography and race."[1] In fact, recent research indicates that children clearly begin to distinguish skin colors and make judgments based on them as early as the preschool years. One experiment conducted at the University of Texas by psychology professor Rebecca Bigler studied the question of when children begin to notice racial differences. The experiment involved children ages four to five and was conducted in three preschool classrooms. The children were divided into two groups and randomly given either a blue or red T-shirt. For three weeks, the children wore these T-shirts. The teachers never mentioned the different colors, nor did they ever separate the children based on shirt color. When playing, the students did not self-segregate by shirt color.

Still, when Bigler later asked the children which group was better to belong to, nearly all of them chose their own color. They also said they believed they were smarter than members of the other group. While some children said that some of the members of the other group were mean, they said that none of the members of their own group were mean. The children had a clear sense of superiority regarding the other group. "The Reds never showed hatred for Blues," said Bigler. "It was more like, 'Blues are fine, but not as good as us.'"[2] Bigler concluded that children will use readily apparent differences, including skin color, to put people into categories and make distinctions between themselves and others. Rather than having to decide for themselves what categories to separate people into, children pick up on the categories that already divide society. Despite all of this evidence, the mistaken belief persists that talking to kids about race will be the factor that makes them start noticing racial differences.

Even white people who identify as antiracist can sometimes fall into the trap of perpetuating their own privilege. Sociologist Margaret Hagerman spent two years in a Midwestern city interviewing and observing 30 families for her book

White Kids: Growing Up With Privilege in a Racially Divided America. In an article for NBC News, Noah Berlatsky wrote:

> as Hagerman told me, "all of these families in their own ways were participating in the reproduction of racial inequality." Children were sent to private school, or when they went to public school benefited from private tutors or enrichment classes. Even community service can reproduce racist ideas. It's hard to see people as equals when you always have power over them, or when your primary experience with them involves giving them charity.[3]

Raising Awareness

In addition to parents, teachers are key figures in shaping a child's attitudes toward others. Just as parents can help prevent racism and promote racial justice through discussions of values and tolerance at home, teachers can do the same in the classroom. There are many classroom activities in use every day that help raise student awareness of racism. These include traditional activities such as reading and responding to poems, short stories, and novels written by people of color that deal with race and racism around the world. However, teachers can also find other ways to make the curriculum less Eurocentric and focus on the contributions of people of color.

Some attempts to increase diversity have been criticized as "slacktivism," or actions taken to make people feel like they're making a difference without actually changing anything. For instance, in early 2020, the bookstore Barnes & Noble announced an initiative called Diverse Editions, in which classic books had been redesigned to have people of color on the covers. The bookstore said its intention was to be more inclusive, but the backlash was so strong that Barnes & Noble ended up canceling the initiative. People expressed anger and disappointment over the fact that, instead of highlighting authors of color, people had taken books by white authors that focus on white culture and that have already received widespread attention for decades—including *Moby Dick*, *The Secret Garden*, *The Wizard of Oz*, and

Students who seek out diversity in their study groups and reading materials are exposed to a wider range of views and tend to become better informed and more open-minded than students who don't.

Frankenstein—and tried to remarket them to people of color. Many felt it was wrong to trick young people of color into thinking a book was about someone who shared their experiences. As author David Bowles explained, "Imagine a black girl ... who picks up a copy of *The Secret Garden* and sees this beautiful black girl on the cover and gets the book and is all excited about it and reads it and realizes it was a book about a white girl who has a racist family and racist beliefs herself."[4]

Addressing Racism

Beyond the home and the classroom, racism can be addressed in the community at large through programs that encourage

The Problem With "Not Seeing Color"

Some people believe that talking about race is itself a racist action. People who hold such views may say they aren't racist because they're figuratively "colorblind," a term they use to mean that they don't notice the color of someone's skin. The intention is to show that they don't base their treatment of anyone on skin color and that they see everyone as equals. They may also talk about how discussing race divides society and ignoring it brings everyone together. However, many people, particularly people of color, have criticized such views. Firstly, because race is an important part of many people's identity, pretending not to notice it can be offensive. Secondly, accusing people who bring up race of being racist or dividing society can make it difficult for people of color to discuss their experiences with racism.

Pretending that race doesn't exist and isn't an issue means that people who claim to be colorblind will often dismiss the idea that any unfair situation is the result of racism. Talking about race is sometimes uncomfortable, but it's impossible to solve a problem by pretending it doesn't exist. Rather than aiming for colorblindness, white people should focus on being good allies to people of color.

racial justice and tolerance. People around the world work to improve race relations through discussion groups, community education programs, and other activities. Founded in 1993, Seeds of Peace is an organization that offers programs in multiple countries to help prevent racism by fostering the development of empathy and respect for others. One program is a yearly summer camp in Maine for young people of all races. There, the participants work on a series of team-building activities with the goal of bringing them in close contact with one another to develop mutual respect and empathy.

Another organization is the People's Institute for Survival and Beyond (PISAB). Founded in 1980, the institute trains people to become effective community organizers. More than 100,000 people have gone through the institute's Undoing Racism Workshop, where they learn the basic skills necessary to lead racial justice activities in their own communities. These include effective community organizing, leadership development, coalition building, fundraising, and publicity. PISAB also conducts a program called the People's Institute Youth Agenda (PIYA). This program mentors young people in universities and throughout the communities in which the institute is active, helping them learn to recognize and speak out against racism while promoting racial justice in their own schools and communities.

While community programs such those offered by Seeds of Peace and PISAB can't completely end all racism, they can begin an important process. Activism and dialogue between people of different backgrounds can lead to a greater awareness of racism and how to take steps to promote racial justice in a community.

Another arena in which there have been efforts to prevent racism is the workplace. In 2018, Starbucks made national headlines when it closed all of its stores for a staff training day about implicit, or unknown, bias and how it contributes to discrimination. This was a direct result of an incident in which a Starbucks employee reported two black men to the police for trespassing as they were waiting in the store for a friend to arrive. Experts say a one-day training course isn't enough to completely erase implicit bias, but it's a step in the right direction.

Another way employers are trying to change is by making a true effort to hire more people of color. Scott E. Page, a professor at the University of Michigan, has spent years researching diversity in the workplace, and he's convinced that an organization's strength lies in its diversity. For Page, productivity, not prejudice, is the focus. Using statistical models, Page determined that a variety of backgrounds working together often produce the best results for a company. "People from different backgrounds have varying ways of looking at problems, what I call 'tools,'" said Page. "The sum of these tools is far more powerful in organizations with diversity than in ones where everyone has gone to the same schools, been trained in the same mold and thinks in almost identical ways."[5]

All of these efforts to prevent racism and promote racial justice at home, in schools, in the workplace, and in the community will determine how strong of a hold racism will continue to have on society. Racist attitudes may never be completely erased, but it may one day be possible to improve society's commitment to justice and equality for people of all races.

Your Opinion Matters!

1. How can white people become better allies to people of color?

2. What policies can schools and businesses put in place to fight racism and promote racial justice?

3. How does diversity benefit schools and companies?

CHAPTER FIVE

WHAT COMES NEXT?

Racism isn't just hatred of people of color. It also covers the ways society is set up to naturally help white people while at the same time working against people of color. This has gone on for so long that most white people don't notice it until it's pointed out to them. Sometimes they deny it because they feel uncomfortable with the idea that they've been profiting from racism—especially if they consider themselves antiracist.

Because racism is so deeply engrained in society, the fight to dismantle it and replace it with a system of racial justice will be long and difficult. It will require people changing their attitudes and actions, which is hard when people are unaware of their biases and impossible when people don't see a problem with their beliefs. White people who are committed to helping end racism and promote racial justice must learn how to be good allies, listen more than they speak, examine their privilege, and be willing to actively work to dismantle a system that's set up to benefit them. Racial justice cannot become a reality when the group in power is afraid of losing the benefits it believes it deserves.

◀ When white people are pulled over by police, they may feel angry or upset, but they generally aren't scared for their lives the way many black people are. This is just one example of white privilege.

Stereotyping Based on Misconceptions

Misunderstandings between people of different races can undermine efforts to deal effectively with racism. A failure to understand a person of a different race can often deepen tensions. For instance, when many Americans think of a terrorist, they picture a brown-skinned, Muslim person—often one who's foreign-born—even though the overwhelming majority of mass shootings, bombings, and similar violent actions in the United States are performed by American-born white men. The fear that everyone with brown skin—including Arabs, Middle Easterners, and Southeast Asians—could potentially be a Muslim terrorist has had several different implications. First, it's caused some people to fear those who identify as Muslim, even though the vast majority of Muslims condemn the actions of radical extremists. Second, it has made some people assume that anyone with brown skin is Muslim, even though people with brown skin come from many different backgrounds and practice a variety of religions.

Sikhism is a religion that's mainly practiced in India. Sikhs believe in one god and promote equality for everyone. However, Sikh men, who wear turbans and long beards as part of their faith, are particular targets because many Americans associate these features with terrorists such as Osama bin Laden, who was the mastermind behind the September 11, 2001, terrorist attacks. According to *The Atlantic*, a nonprofit group called the Sikh Coalition "found that two-thirds of Sikh students get bullied at school. Students reported being accused of hiding grenades or bombs under their head coverings … In a group of 180 students surveyed in Fresno, California, a third said they were bullied because their peers thought they look like terrorists."[1] Surveys by a group called the Stanford Peace Innovation Lab found that 49 percent of Americans mistakenly believe Sikh is a sect, or group, of Islam, and 79 percent are unaware that Sikhism was started in India, not the Middle East.

This focus on people from South Asia or the Middle East as the image of a terrorist harms innocent people and doesn't take into account the fact that homegrown terrorist organizations

Radical Islamist Osama bin Laden was considered one of the most dangerous enemies of the United States until a group of Navy SEALS killed him in 2011. Many Americans associate his turban and beard with terrorists, even though most terrorists wear neither.

advocating white supremacy and an extreme form of nationalism are a rapidly growing and greater threat to US citizens than foreign-based organizations struggling halfway around the world. New America, a public policy think tank, reported that of the 15 people who carried out deadly radical Islamist attacks in the United States since September 11, 2001, all were American citizens or legal residents. Several were born in the United States; most were born into families that had come from places such as Palestine, Afghanistan, and Egypt, but three were African American, two were Russian, and two were white Americans—one born in Texas, the other born in Florida. However, radical Islamists are in the minority when it comes to American terrorism. Far more terrorist attacks have been carried out by white supremacist groups, anti-government groups, Christian anti-abortion groups, and animal rights groups.

Fear of a particular group makes it more difficult to fight racism because people tend not to have an interest in getting to know someone they're afraid of. Avoiding someone out of fear makes it impossible to overcome negative stereotypes. For this reason, people have been encouraging others to get to know Muslims. A woman named Tara Miele interviewed several Muslims for a short YouTube video called "Meet a Muslim," and Aysha Yaqoob, a student at the University of Regina in Saskatchewan, Canada, held a "Meet a Muslim" event at her school. Miele, Yaqoob, and others like them hope to give people an opportunity to challenge and broaden their views of Muslims so there's less hatred directed at them and others who are perceived to be Muslim.

Presidential Influence

When Barack Obama was elected president, many people were hopeful that he would be able to create policies to help people of color, especially other black people, gain more equality. However, according to Melissa Harris-Lacewell, an associate professor of politics and African American studies at Princeton University in New Jersey, "the election of a black president has not changed the material realities of racial inequality. African-Americans are significantly more distressed than their white counterparts on every meaningful economic indicator: income, unemployment, wealth, education, home ownership and home foreclosures."[2]

Obama also faced racism directed at him. After his election in 2008, some people protested him and his administration with racist messages, such as telling him to go back to Kenya, even though he's a US citizen. Throughout all eight years of his presidency, he faced accusations that he wasn't born in the United States; if this had been proven true, he would have had to step down as president, since the president must be born in the country. Donald Trump was one of Obama's most vocal critics, demanding that Obama show the public his birth certificate to prove he was a natural-born citizen. Even after Obama produced proof that he had been born in Hawai'i, Trump and others continued to attack him, claiming that his birth certificate was fake.

President Trump has also had protests directed at him, but it isn't because of the color of his skin. Most of the protests have been in response to perceived racist, sexist, and xenophobic (fear or hatred of foreigners) statements he has made. After he signed an executive order in January 2017 restricting immigration to the United States from some Muslim-majority countries, protests sprang up around the United States. Some people went to major airports to show their support for refugees and immigrants. The executive order's "travel ban" was referred to as a "Muslim ban" by opponents. Trump's supporters pointed out that his executive order never mentioned the word "Muslim" and said the ban was necessary to prevent terrorists from posing as immigrants and coming into the country. However, since Islam is the majority religion in the affected countries, the order does mean that Muslims are the ones most affected.

The executive order has been criticized for several reasons. Firstly, although the executive order talked about the terrorist attacks of September 11, 2001, the countries where those terrorists came from were not included in the ban. Some have accused Trump of leaving them out because he has business dealings

Many people who have supported Trump's travel ban do so because they believe Islam is a violent religion. In reality, like Christianity, it preaches peace.

there, but the White House denied this, stating that the countries were chosen based on a list made by the Obama administration.

Secondly, the ban has been widely criticized as racist because it implies that everyone from the countries on the list is a potential threat, despite the fact that research has shown this fear is unfounded: According to the CATO Institute, an American has a 0.00003 percent chance of dying in an attack carried out by a foreign-born terrorist. They have a much higher chance of being killed in a car crash.

Thirdly, athough terrorism is a serious issue, many people believe that, rather than making Americans safer, the only effect the ban will have is to harm people who are fleeing war and terrorism in their own countries, particularly Syria. It has been compared to US policies that denied entry to Jews who were fleeing Nazi Germany during World War II. Critics argue that other issues, such as gun control, should be a more important focus and that the only reason for the ban is a racist fear of people from Muslim-majority countries.

Finally, the ban has been called unconstitutional because the United States has separation of church and state, which means laws are not supposed to be made that give preference to or actively target any particular religion. The Supreme Court struck down the travel ban in 2017, but it upheld a later version of the ban on June 26, 2018. This version allowed people from the affected countries to apply for a waiver if they wanted to come to the United States. However, critics have stated that the waiver process is unfairly implemented. One lawsuit stated that 14 waiver applicants have been under consideration for their waiver for 18 months and have yet to receive a clear answer about whether they'll be granted entry to the United States. As of 2020, the travel ban is still in effect, although people are still trying to fight it in court.

Will Racial Mixing End Racism?

Anthropologist Nina Jablonski imagined a future in which race remains a fact of life, but fewer distinctions based on race

Different Perspectives

Sometimes people disagree on whether something is racist or empowering based on their personal perspective. One example is the movie *Crazy Rich Asians*. Many Americans, especially Asian Americans, applauded the release of a Hollywood movie focused entirely on Asians, who are frequently overlooked by mainstream American society. The movie showed the main characters as being rich and powerful, and they're sometimes shown using these advantages to fight racism against them.

However, in Singapore, where the movie is set, the reception was very different. Many people noted that the rich and powerful Asians in the film are Chinese and that the few South Asian characters are mainly portrayed as servants. In a country where Chinese people already hold most of the power and darker-skinned Asians are often discriminated against, many viewers did not find this movie empowering. Furthermore, as author Fatima Bhutto noted, "it is the monoculture of capitalism, not Asia, that is on display. In fact, 'Asia' is used [in the movie] in the same manner that many westerners employ 'Africa,' lumping together 48 countries with distinct cultures, languages, and histories … Asianness is mere window dressing."[1]

1. Fatima Bhutto, "Crazy Rich Asians Is No Racial Triumph. It's a Soulless Salute to the 1%," *Guardian*, September 12, 2018, www.theguardian.com/film/2018/sep/12/crazy-rich-asians-racial-triumph.

exist, especially as interracial marriage becomes more common and socially accepted. Complexion, or skin tone, is already a complicated subject. People who identify themselves as white may have genetically darker skin than many white people, whereas self-identifying black people may appear lighter than some white people. Colorism is also a problem. This is when people—sometimes even people within the same race—discriminate against each other based on skin color. For example, a dark-skinned black person will often encounter more racism than a light-skinned black person and may even be discriminated against by light-skinned black people. Scholar Henry Louis Gates

Shown here is famous musician and civil rights activist Nina Simone. Much of her musical work centered around her experiences as a dark-skinned black woman, which were much different than those of light-skinned black women.

Jr. said "race" is a relative term. All people, he suggested, are of mixed race, products of a complicated history. "The more we use DNA tests to trace our family trees, the more we're going to discover just how tangled our roots really are," said Gates. "We are all mulattoes [biracial people] of one kind or another. In the end, what actually makes us black or white? Or have those terms become outdated?"[3]

The answer to Gates's question may lie within the recent work of geneticists. Scientists have mapped the human genome, the complex code of human life, and determined that all human beings are basically genetically the same. Race, therefore, is simply a social construct with no basis in science. Any differences between races are likely a result of historical developments, such as wars, slavery, migration patterns, and agriculture. In tracing human history to its very roots, scientists have also concluded that all human beings originated on the African continent around 200,000 years ago. Thus, a common ancestor may connect all of humanity. Skin color is also an adaptation; over thousands of years, people developed the best skin color to suit their environment. People in warmer climates, such as Africa and India, have darker skin because it protects them from sunburn; people in colder climates, such as Norway, have lighter skin because it helps them absorb enough sunlight to produce vitamin D even during the dark winter months. These traits developed over millions of years and are passed on genetically, so even if someone moves from one type of climate to another, their skin color won't change very much.

Despite the scientific proof that racial differences are genetically meaningless, some people remain convinced that races are categories that can be used to understand human behavior, morality, or intelligence. In the United States and other countries around the world, defining people by the color of their skin is a kind of shorthand by which people are viewed and often judged, for better and for worse, and it continues to influence life, especially in the world of education.

An Unreliable Test

Some companies, including Ancestry DNA, 23andMe, and Family Tree DNA, offer genetic tests to help people discover their ancestry. Sometimes people are surprised by the results; for instance, when Pearl Duncan, a black woman, took the test, it told her she was 10 percent Scottish. DNA tests are relatively expensive, but for people who are willing to pay, the test can be a fun experiment.

However, experts caution against taking DNA tests as proof of ancestry. Since race is a socially created idea, there is no gene that determines it. *Slate* magazine explained:

> *Our genes dictate certain things about us—there's a gene that programs the color of your eyes, for example. But ethnicity is not a trait derived from a single gene, because ethnicity is mostly our perception of a collection of traits, rather than a trait itself. So a genetic test that looks at our genes and comes back with an assessment of our ethnic roots isn't honing in on a specific gene and reading what it says because there's no such gene to read. Instead, the test is comparing snippets of our DNA to snippets of DNA of people of known origin and looking for similarities.*

> *The problem is that DNA snippets, or markers, are inconsistent. Sometimes they are passed on and sometimes they are not, and whether they are or aren't is random ... So when a DNA test comes back saying you are 28 percent Finnish, all it's really saying is that of the DNA analyzed ... 28 percent of it was most similar to that of a completely Finnish person. In the end, these comparisons are a fun but ultimately unreliable way to think about the possibilities of [who] your ancestors might have been, rather than definitive proof of your ethnic background.*[1]

1. Matt Miller, "A DNA Test Won't Explain Elizabeth Warren's Ancestry," *Slate*, June 29, 2016, www.slate.com/articles/technology/future_tense/2016/06/ dna_testing_cannot_determine_ancestry_including_elizabeth_warren_s.html.

Still Fighting School Segregation

Many American schools legally separated black students from white ones until the 1954 *Brown v. Board of Education of Topeka* Supreme Court decision made the practice illegal. However, some schools remain segregated today because school officials "do not know the status of their desegregation orders, have never read them, or erroneously [wrongly] believe that orders have been ended."[4] Some people don't believe segregation is a problem, but research has shown that "desegregated schools are linked to important benefits, like prejudice reduction, heightened civic engagement and analytical thinking, and better learning outcomes in general."[5] Students who have a chance to interact with people who are different than them will learn more and become better informed about racial and cultural issues.

Although schools can't legally be segregated by refusing entry to students of color, many are de facto segregated. This means many schools are either overwhelmingly white or overwhelmingly nonwhite due to factors such as where students live, how much their families make, and how easy it is for them to travel to school. For example, a poor black family may be unable to afford to send their child to a private school. Even if they can, it might be difficult or impossible for the student to get there; their family might not have a car, and there might not be buses that go from the child's neighborhood to the school. Because people of color are disproportionately likely to live in poverty, they're also disproportionately likely to attend public schools with other low-income students. This affects the schools and the quality of the children's education for a number of reasons: "They are in poorer communities, they have less local resources, they have fewer parents with college degrees, they have fewer two parent families where there are parents who can come spend time volunteering in the school, they have a harder time attracting the best teachers."[6]

While some people believe there is no longer a need for forced integration in schools like there was in 1954, Rita Jones Turner doesn't agree. In 1970, she became one of the first black students to attend Vestavia Hills High School in Birmingham, Alabama, after forced desegregation. She remembered that often the school bus wouldn't stop on her street; when it did and she arrived at school, she was placed into remedial classes even though she didn't need extra help. At lunchtime, white students harassed her, making her learning environment hostile.

Thirty-six years later, Jones Turner received a note from her old school informing her of its attempt to change the policy of desegregation and force her ninth-grade son to enroll elsewhere. Specifically, the school district filed a court motion to stop forced integration. Jones Turner's own experience at Vestavia Hills remained a painful memory, but she resented any attempts at turning back the clock on progress. "We were used, mistreated, downtrodden, and discriminated against," said Jones Turner. "I have no problem with being a sacrificial lamb for the good of the community, but to have the system back out now is not fair. They made a commitment to educate black children."[7]

The Vestavia Hills school board denied any racial motivation in wanting to halt integration; instead, the board claimed that economics forced their decision. The school said its budget could no longer bear the strain of busing black students from all the way across town. A judge ruled in favor of the school.

School segregation affects more than just schools. According to writer Roger Shuler, "The euphemism you hear in the Birmingham real-estate game is that cities such as Mountain Brook, Vestavia Hills, and Homewood have 'good schools.' That means they have overwhelmingly white schools, and many home buyers are willing to pay hugely inflated prices to live in those areas."[8] The rising cost of housing means many families of color cannot afford to live in those areas, so they cannot send their children to those schools.

The Future of Race Relations

After Trump's election in 2016, some white people expressed shock; they assumed he would lose the election because of his perceived racist, sexist, and xenophobic comments. However, according to the *New York Times*, "when … black Americans were interviewed recently about Mr. Trump's candidacy, shock was rarely a word that came to mind. More often, they said, what they felt was a numbing familiarity: What the rest of America was now being exposed to are words and thoughts they have heard their whole lives."[9]

Although racism against black people has been prominent in the news, especially after the start of the BLM movement, other groups who experience racism are rarely talked about. Data from the Centers for Disease Control and Prevention (CDC) that was "collected from medical examiners in 47 states between 1999 and 2011" found that "[w]hen compared to their percentage of the U.S. population, Natives were more likely to be killed by police than any other group, including African Americans."[10] However, the US media rarely reports these killings. Although BLM has received much media attention, a similar initiative called Native Lives Matter, started in 2014, has gone almost entirely unreported. According to Lydia Millet, a writer for the *New York Times*, "When it comes to American Indians, mainstream America suffers from willful blindness."[11] Some would rather not hear about issues such as these because it makes them feel sad, frustrated, or defensive. However, ignoring problems doesn't make them disappear.

Racism against Asians is also rarely spoken about, and because the mainstream perception of Asians is generally positive, many people deny that it exists. However, racial slurs and microaggressions are commonly directed at people in this racial group, and they're largely ignored in the media. This lack of attention to Asians and any problems they may be facing is itself a form of racism.

Bias based on race has not faded, but it has been complicated by the addition of bias based on religion, especially a religion practiced mainly by people of a certain race. Jews, Muslims, and people who are mistaken for members of both groups have been the targets of hate crimes for years, but the intensity of people's fear and hatred seems to have increased since the turn of the

Some people dress as Native Americans for Halloween, and the costumes are frequently historically inaccurate. Using another race's culture as a costume—especially while ignoring them in the present day—is racist.

millennium. Fears about nonwhite immigrants have also en-hanced the racism toward Latinx that has existed for many years. No one can say for certain whether racism will ever be entirely destroyed, but progress toward racial justice can continue to be made as long as people of all races keep speaking out against rac-ism and standing up for each other. As noted social rights activist Desmond Tutu pointed out, "If you are neutral in situations of injustice, you have chosen the side of the oppressor."[12]

Your Opinion Matters!

1. How are Islamophobia and anti-Semitism similar to racism? How are they different?

2. What does racial justice mean to you?

3. Do you think racism can ever be completely eliminated? Why or why not?

The following are some suggestions for taking what you've just read and applying that information to your everyday life.

- Confront racism when you see it happening.

- Call others out on racist remarks even if no one of that race is close enough to hear.

- Make an effort to include people of all races in group events, such as school projects, parties, and lunch tables. However, don't insist that someone join your group just for the sake of creating diversity.

- Treat everyone with respect regardless of their skin color or religion.

- Work to understand how race and religion shape another person's worldview. Don't tell them to stop talking so much about it. Ask questions if you don't understand something, but do so in a way that's respectful.

- Apologize if you offend someone, and resist the urge to explain why you said what you did. People can still be offended even if no offense was meant.

- Make an effort to notice your privilege in everyday life, and do what you can to level the playing field for others who have less privilege.

- Be critical of news stories and the way they portray people of color versus white people.

- Listen to the stories people of color tell, and make an effort to understand their point of view. However, don't compare their struggle to your own life.

- If you're white, understand that you don't have to be included in everything and that organizations specifically for people of color aren't racist. When you're asked not to involve yourself in something, respect that request without complaining.

- If you're a person of color, talk to trusted adults. Ask for their guidance about how to deal with racism when it's directed at you and how to keep yourself safe.

- Learn more about microaggressions and how to avoid them. Remember that even people of color can commit microaggressions against each other without meaning to.

- Read books and articles written by people of color.

- Ask your parents' permission to attend a protest about a cause that affects people of color. Research the cause beforehand to understand what you're protesting.

- Don't expect to be praised or thanked for your actions. Do something because it's the right thing to do, not because you want to portray a certain image of yourself.

Introduction: A Long History of Hate

1. "Institutional Racism," Racism. No Way!, 2015, www.racismnoway.com.au/teaching-resources/factsheets/32.html.

2. Andrea Alvarez, e-mail interview by author, March 9, 2020.

3. Ernest Allen Jr. and Robert Chrisman, "Ten Reasons: A Response to David Horowitz," *Black Scholar* 31, no. 2 (2001).

Chapter One: What Does Racism Look Like?

1. Quoted in Beverly Daniel Tatum, *"Why Are All the Black Kids Sitting Together in the Cafeteria?" And Other Conversations About Race* (New York, NY: Basic Books, 1999), p. 7.

2. Niall McCarthy, "Report: Trump's Election Led to a Surge in Hate Crimes [Infographic]," *Forbes*, November 30, 2016, www.forbes.com/sites/niallmccarthy/2016/11/30/report-trumps-election-led-to-a-surge-in-hate-crime-infographic.

3. Quoted in Katya Adler, "Spain Reflects on Football Racism Row," BBC News, November 18, 2004, news.bbc.co.uk/2/hi/europe/4024167.stm.

4. Quoted in Rachel Donadio, "Race Riots Grip Italian Town, and Mafia Is Suspected," *New York Times*, January 10, 2010, www.nytimes.com/2010/01/11/world/europe/11italy.html.

5. Quoted in Dan Gilgoff, "Investing in Diversity," *U.S. News & World Report*, November 1, 2009, p. 72.

6. "School-to-Prison Pipeline," ACLU, accessed February 13, 2020, www.aclu.org/issues/juvenile-justice/school-prison-pipeline.

7. "School-to-Prison Pipeline," ACLU.

8. Quoted in Heben Nigatu, "21 Racial Microaggressions You Hear on a Daily Basis," BuzzFeed, December 9, 2013, www.buzzfeed.com/hnigatu/racial-microagressions-you-hear-on-a-daily-basis.

9. Molefi Kete Asante, *Erasing Racism: The Survival of the American Nation* (Amherst, NY: Prometheus Books, 2009), p. 254.

10. Sharon H. Chang, "Opinion: Closure of POC Yoga Due to Hate, Death Threats a Tragedy for All People of Color," *International Examiner*, October 18, 2015, www.iexaminer.org/2015/10/poc-yoga-closure-a-tragedy.

Chapter Two: What Causes Racism?

1. *Modern Family*, season 6, episode 7, "Queer Eyes, Full Hearts," directed by Jason Winer, written by Stephen Lloyd, aired November 12, 2014.

2. "Racism and Psychology," American Psychological Association. Brochure.

3. Quoted in "Maryland Police Question U.S. Citizen's Immigration Status," CBS News, January 28, 2017, www.cbsnews.com/news/maryland-police-question-us-citizen-immigration-status.

4. Camila Domonoske and Bill Chappell, "Minnesota Gov. Calls Traffic Stop Shooting 'Absolutely Appalling at All Levels,'" *Two-Way*, NPR, July 7, 2016, www.npr.org/sections/thetwo-way/2016/07/07/485066807/police-stop-ends-in-black-mans-death-aftermath-is-livestreamed-online-video.

5. Shawn Regan, "5 Ways the Government Keeps Native Americans in Poverty," *Forbes*, March 13, 2014, www.forbes.com/sites/real-spin/2014/03/13/5-ways-the-government-keeps-native-americans-in-poverty.

6. Quoted in Huizhong Wu, "The 'Model Minority' Myth: Why Asian-American Poverty Goes Unseen," Mashable, December 14, 2015, mashable.com/2015/12/14/asian-american-poverty.

Chapter Three: Resistance to Change

1. Nadra Kareem Nittle, "A Guide to Understanding and Avoiding Cultural Appropriation," ThoughtCo., modified July 3, 2019,

www.thoughtco.com/cultural-appropriation-and-why-iits-wrong-2834561.

2. Adrienne K., "But Why Can't I Wear a Hipster Headdress?" Native Appropriations, April 27, 2010, nativeappropriations.com/2010/04/but-why-cant-i-wear-a-hipster-headdress.html.

3. Anjali Joshi, "Why a Bindi is NOT an Example of Cultural Appropriation," *HuffPost*, modified December 6, 2017, www.huffpost.com/entry/why-a-bindi-is-not-an-exa_b_5150693.

4. Quoted in "Document: Commencement Address at Howard University: 'To Fulfill These Rights,'" Teaching American History, accessed February 14, 2020, teachingamericanhistory.org/library/document/commencement-address-at-howard-university-to-fulfill-these-rights.

5. Quoted in Linda Greenhouse, *Becoming Justice Blackmun: Harry Blackmun's Supreme Court Journey* (New York: Times Books, 2005), p. 133.

6. John Blake, "This Is What 'Whitelash' Looks Like," CNN, November 19, 2016, www.cnn.com/2016/11/11/us/obama-trump-white-backlash.

Chapter Four: Fighting Against Racism

1. Sean McElwee, "The Hidden Racism of Young White Americans," PBS *NewsHour*, March 24, 2015, www.pbs.org/newshour/updates/americas-racism-problem-far-complicated-think.

2. Quoted in Po Bronson and Ashley Merryman, "Even Babies Discriminate: A Nurtureshock Excerpt," *Newsweek*, September 4, 2009, www.newsweek.com/even-babies-discriminate-nurtureshock-excerpt-79233.

3. Noah Berlatsky, "White Kids, Racism and the Way Privileged Parenting Props Up an Unjust System," NBC News, January 2, 2019, www.nbcnews.com/think/opinion/white-kids-racism-way-privileged-parenting-props-unjust-system-ncna953951.

4. Quoted in Kara Yorio, "Diverse Editions Pulled Before Release; Author David Bowles, Others, Speak Out Against New Covers of 'Classics,'" *School Library Journal*, February 5, 2020, www.slj.com/?detailStory=-

diverse-editions-pulled-before-release-author-david-bowles-others-speak-out-against-new-covers-on-Classics.

5. Quoted in Claudia Dreifus, "In Professor's Model, Diversity = Productivity," *New York Times*, January 8, 2008, www.nytimes.com/2008/01/08/science/08conv.html.

Chapter Five: What Comes Next?

1. Emma Green, "The Trouble with Wearing Turbans in America," *The Atlantic*, January 27, 2015, www.theatlantic.com/politics/archive/2015/01/the-trouble-with-wearing-turbans-in-america/384832.

2. Melissa Harris-Lacewell, "Commentary: Racial Progress Is Far from Finished," CNN, June 5, 2009, edition.cnn.com/2009/LIVING/07/07/lacewell.post.racial/index.html.

3. Quoted in Ashlinn Quinn, "'Rationalizing Race in US History,'" *African American Lives* 2, PBS, www.pbs.org/wnet/aalives/teachers/rationalizing_race.html.

4. Nikole Hannah-Jones, "School Districts Still Face Fights—and Confusion—on Integration," *The Atlantic*, May 2, 2014, www.theatlantic.com/education/archive/2014/05/lack-of-order-the-erosion-of-a-once-great-force-for-integration/361563.

5. Lauren Camera, "The New Segregation," *U.S. News & World Report*, July 26, 2016, www.usnews.com/news/articles/2016-07-26/racial-tensions-flare-as-schools-resegregate.

6. Janie Boschma and Ronald Brownstein, "The Concentration of Poverty in American Schools," *The Atlantic*, February 29, 2016, www.theatlantic.com/education/archive/2016/02/concentration-poverty-american-schools/471414.

7. Quoted in Jenny Jarvie, "'It Feels Like We're Back in the '60s,'" *Los Angeles Times*, October 22, 2006, www.latimes.com/archives/la-xpm-2006-oct-22-na-deseg22-story.html.

8. Roger Shuler, "School Segregation Is Taking New Forms," *Daily Kos*, January 29, 2010, www.dailykos.com/story/2010/1/29/831859/-.

9. Yamiche Alcindor, "Black Voters on Donald Trump: We've Heard

It All Before," *New York Times*, October 25, 2016, www.nytimes.
com/2016/10/26/us/politics/donald-trump-black-voters.html.

10. Stephanie Woodard, "The Police Killings No One Is Talking About,"
In These Times, October 17, 2016, inthesetimes.com/features/native_
american_police_killings_native_lives_matter.html.

11. Lydia Millet, "Native Lives Matter, Too," *New York Times*, October 13,
2015, www.nytimes.com/2015/10/13/opinion/native-lives-matter-too.
html.

12. Quoted in Erin Cossetta, "23 Quotes That Perfectly Explain Racism
(To People Who Don't 'See Color')," *Thought Catalog*, May 1, 2014,
thoughtcatalog.com/erin-cossetta/2014/04/quotes-that-perfectly-
explain-racism-to-people-who-dont-see-color.

FOR MORE INFORMATION

Books: Nonfiction

Cruz, Bárbara. *The Fight for Latino Civil Rights*. New York, NY: Enslow Publishing, 2016.

Houston, Jeanne Wakatsuki, and James D. Houston. *Farewell to Manzanar*. New York, NY: Houghton Mifflin, 1973.

Leatherboy, Mary Beth, and Lisa Charleyboy. *Urban Tribes: Native Americans in the City*. Toronto, ON, Canada: Annick Press, 2015.

Robinson, Chuck. *Racism*. Philadelphia, PA: Mason Crest, 2017.

Books: Fiction

Ahmed, Samira. *Internment*. New York, NY: Little, Brown and Company, 2019.

Thomas, Angie. *The Hate U Give*. New York, NY: HarperCollins, 2017.

Websites

Let's Fight Racism!

www.un.org/en/letsfightracism

This website, a project of the United Nations, gives people the opportunity to learn more about different racial groups to decrease the fear and ignorance that lead to racism.

Project Implicit

implicit.harvard.edu/implicit/takeatest.html

Taking an IAT can be an interesting way to discover biases you may not know you have about race, gender, sexuality, age, and more. However, researchers note that the test doesn't give accurate results if it's taken just once.

Race: The Power of an Illusion

www.pbs.org/race/001_WhatIsRace/001_00-home.htm

This section of the PBS website includes activities that help people gain a better understanding of race and racism.

Showing Up for Racial Justice

www.showingupforracialjustice.org

This campaign helps white people organize to show support for their local racial justice groups.

Teaching Tolerance

www.tolerance.org

This website is a project of the Southern Poverty Law Center. It features a wide range of resources that encourage understanding and acceptance among races.

Organizations

American Civil Liberties Union (ACLU)
125 Broad Street, 18th Floor
New York, NY 10004
www.aclu.org
www.instagram.com/aclu_nationwide
twitter.com/aclu
www.youtube.com/aclu
Founded in 1920, the ACLU protects the rights of Americans from overreach by schools, businesses, and the government.

Amnesty International (USA Headquarters)
5 Penn Plaza, 16th Floor
New York, NY 10001
www.amnestyusa.org
www.instagram.com/amnestyusa
twitter.com/amnestyusa
youtube.com/amnestyusa
Amnesty International is a worldwide organization that campaigns for internationally recognized human rights for all. The organization's supporters work to end injustice and to improve human rights through campaigning and international solidarity. The US chapter focuses on injustice specifically in the United States.

Human Rights Watch
350 Fifth Avenue, 34th Floor
New York, NY 10118
www.hrw.org
www.instagram.com/humanrightswatch
twitter.com/hrw
www.youtube.com/user/HumanRightsWatch
As one of the world's leading independent defenders and protectors of human rights, Human Rights Watch works to focus international attention where human rights are being violated.

**National Association for the Advancement
of Colored People (NAACP)**
4805 Mt. Hope Drive
Baltimore, MD 21215
www.naacp.org
www.instagram.com/naacp
twitter.com/NAACP
www.youtube.com/user/naacpvideos/videos
Founded in 1909, the NAACP has championed social justice and
fought for the civil rights of black people for more than a century.

The People's Institute for Survival and Beyond (PISAB)
601 North Carrollton Avenue
New Orleans, LA 70119
www.pisab.org
twitter.com/UndoingRacism
This national and international collective of antiracist,
multicultural community organizers and educators is dedicated
to building an effective movement for social transformation
through its Undoing Racism workshops. The institute helps
individuals, communities, organizations, and institutions
address the causes of racism in order to create a fairer and more
equitable society.

Sophie Washburne has been a freelance writer and editor of young adult and adult books for more than 10 years. She travels extensively with her husband, Alan. When they are not traveling, they live in Wales with their cat, Zoe. Sophie enjoys doing crafts and cooking when she has spare time.